PERSPECTIVES ON WRITING
Series Editors, Susan H. McLeod and Rich Rice

PERSPECTIVES ON WRITING
Series Editors, Susan H. McLeod and Rich Rice

The Perspectives on Writing series addresses writing studies in a broad sense. Consistent with the wide ranging approaches characteristic of teaching and scholarship in writing across the curriculum, the series presents works that take divergent perspectives on working as a writer, teaching writing, administering writing programs, and studying writing in its various forms.

The WAC Clearinghouse and Parlor Press are collaborating so that these books will be widely available through free digital distribution and low-cost print editions. The publishers and the Series editor are teachers and researchers of writing, committed to the principle that knowledge should freely circulate. We see the opportunities that new technologies have for further democratizing knowledge. And we see that to share the power of writing is to share the means for all to articulate their needs, interest, and learning into the great experiment of literacy.

Recent Books in the Series

Theresa Lillis, Kathy Harrington, Mary R. Lea, and Sally Mitchell (Eds.), *Working with Academic Literacies: Case Studies Towards Transformative Practice* (2015)

Asao B. Inoue, *Antiracist Writing Assessment Ecologies: An Approach to Teaching and Assessing Writing for a Socially Just Future* (2015)

Beth L. Hewett and Kevin Eric DePew (Eds.), *Foundational Practices of Online Writing Instruction* (2015)

Christy I. Wenger, *Yoga Minds, Writing Bodies: Contemplative Writing Pedagogy* (2015)

Sarah Allen, *Beyond Argument: Essaying as a Practice of (Ex)Change* (2015)

Steven J. Corbett, *Beyond Dichotomy: Synergizing Writing Center and Classroom Pedagogies* (2015)

Tara Roeder and Roseanne Gatto (Eds.), *Critical Expressivism: Theory and Practice in the Composition Classroom* (2014)

Terry Myers Zawacki and Michelle Cox (Eds), *WAC and Second-Language Writers: Research Towards Linguistically and Culturally Inclusive Programs and Practices*, (2014)

Charles Bazerman, *A Rhetoric of Literate Action: Literate Action Volume 1* (2013)

Charles Bazerman, *A Theory of Literate Action: Literate Action Volume 2* (2013)

PLACING THE HISTORY OF COLLEGE WRITING: STORIES FROM THE INCOMPLETE ARCHIVE

Nathan Shepley

The WAC Clearinghouse
wac.colostate.edu
Fort Collins, Colorado

Parlor Press
www.parlorpress.com
Anderson, South Carolina

The WAC Clearinghouse, Fort Collins, Colorado 80523

Parlor Press, 3015 Brackenberry Drive, Anderson, South Carolina 29621

© 2016 by Nathan Shepley. This work is licensed under a Creative Commons Attribution-NonCommercial-NoDerivatives 4.0 International.

Printed in the United States of America

Library of Congress Cataloging-in-Publication Data

Names: Shepley, Nathan, 1981- author.
Title: Placing the history of college writing : stories from the incomplete archive / Nathan Shepley.
Description: Perspectives on writing. | Anderson, South Carolina ; Fort Collins, Colorado Parlor Press, [2016] | Includes bibliographical references.
Identifiers: LCCN 2016001110| ISBN 9781602358010 (pbk. : alk. paper) | ISBN 9781602358027 (hardcover : alk. paper)
Subjects: LCSH: English language--Rhetoric--Study and teaching. | English language--Grammar, Generative--Study and teaching. | Report writing--Study and teaching (Higher)
Classification: LCC PE1403 .S56 2016 | DDC 808/.042071173--dc23
LC record available at http://lccn.loc.gov/2016001110

Copyeditor: Julia Smith
Designer: Mike Palmquist
Series Editor: Susan H. McLeod

This book is printed on acid-free paper.

The WAC Clearinghouse supports teachers of writing across the disciplines. Hosted by Colorado State University, it brings together scholarly journals and book series as well as resources for teachers who use writing in their courses. This book is available in digital format for free download at http://wac.colostate.edu.

Parlor Press, LLC is an independent publisher of scholarly and trade titles in print and multimedia formats. This book is available in print and digital formats from Parlor Press at http://www.parlorpress.com. For submission information or to find out about Parlor Press publications, write to Parlor Press, 3015 Brackenberry Drive, Anderson, South Carolina 29621, or email editor@parlorpress.com.

CONTENTS

List of Illustrations vii
Acknowledgments ix
Chapter One. Placing History, Historicizing Place 3
Chapter Two. Customizing Composition: Students Broadening
Behavioral Codes 25
Chapter Three. Tracking Lines of Communication: Student
Writing as a Response to Civic Issues 51
Chapter Four. Composition on Display: Students Performing
College Competence 77
Chapter Five. Rethinking Links Between Histories
of Composition 95
Chapter Six. Composition as Literacy, Discourse, and Rhetoric 121
Works Cited 137
Glossary 149

LIST OF ILLUSTRATIONS

Figure 1. Ohio University Class of 1873. 32
Figure 2. *The Cougar*, April 1929 44
Figure 3. First page of Albert Farias' "I Live in America,"
The Harvest, 1941. 68
Figure 4. English Department of the Ohio University
College of Education, *Athena*, 1923 107
Figure 5. English Department of the Ohio University
College of Liberal Arts, *Athena*, 1923. 109

ACKNOWLEDGMENTS

Many people influenced the writing of this book and deserve my thanks. In Ohio, Sherrie Gradin and Mara Holt, among others, gave thoughtful feedback on a drastically different version of the manuscript. William (Bill) Kimok and the other archivists at Ohio University's Robert E. and Jean R. Mahn Center for Archives and Special Collections guided me toward some of the primary sources that I analyzed for this work and ensured that I had access to needed texts even when I was far away. In Houston, Paul Butler listened patiently to my evolving ideas about this project and gave insightful suggestions, as did Margot Backus regarding one of my middle chapters. Other people, including James Thomas Zebroski, expressed support for my historical research well before it reached a national audience. The staff of the Archives and Special Collections of the University of Houston generously assisted with locating and copying archived sources. Additionally, Susan McLeod provided clear editorial guidance, and the Perspectives on Writing series' two anonymous outside readers gave recommendations that strengthened my project overall. Last, I am delighted that my grandfather, Joe L. Estes, Jr., is able to see this work in print given that my interest in and esteem of higher education stem partly from his influence.

Another version of the Ohio half of Chapter Two formed one section in my article "When the Margins Move: Lessons from the Writing of One University's First Female Graduate," published in *Open Words: Access and English Studies* (vol. 8, issue 1), so thanks goes to that journal's coeditor, John Tassoni, for letting me publish the new version here. The same goes for Byron Hawk, who let me revise substantially and publish, in Chapter Four, my article "Rhetorical-Ecological Links in Composition History," which originally appeared in *Enculturation* (vol. 15). Too, I would like to thank Sara Webb-Sunderhaus and Kim Donehower, coeditors of *Re-Reading Appalachia: Literacy, Place, and Cultural Resistance*, for giving me permission me to publish, in the Ohio half of Chapter Three, reorganized and theoretically reframed research from my chapter "Place-Conscious Literacy Practices in One Ohio College Town" in their book.

A Martha Gano Houstoun Research Grant in Literary Criticism awarded by the University of Houston Department of English provided generous financial support for archival visits and photocopying. Chapter Three in particular benefited from the scrutiny allowed by multiple research trips.

PLACING THE HISTORY OF COLLEGE WRITING: STORIES FROM THE INCOMPLETE ARCHIVE

CHAPTER ONE
PLACING HISTORY, HISTORICIZING PLACE

This is a book that asks those of us who teach and study writing, especially college-level writing, to scrutinize how the locations of our work matter. I say locations, plural, to stress that we teach not in an environment that must be understood in a single way, but in environments formed by discursive options and by social, economic, and political negotiations, large and small, to say nothing of material factors bearing on where college student writing occurs. We teach in institutions that are governed in a certain fashion and steered toward certain goals, perhaps aligned with the goals of other institutions, educational or otherwise. We teach in towns or cities, neighborhoods, and political districts whose borders can shift with the will of a populace or a set of leaders. We teach in classrooms and, increasingly, in configurations such as writing studios and online forums. And we teach among colleagues and students who import learned attitudes about writing, education, and the world. Even if we perform our teaching in one campus building or help one group of students over several semesters, we teach in many places.

The same ideas apply to the history of college student writing. Even if traced to actions taken in a given year and at an institutional site, historical student writing need not be understood merely as a product of students' interactions with one and only one place, a classroom, and with one and only one kind of engagement, an assignment. In the 1800s and 1900s, American cities, towns, institutions, and writing classrooms changed continually in accordance with changes in the teachers and students populating the classes and with the larger societal needs served by the classes. Influencing and influenced by social, political, and institutional changes were alterations in the discourse surrounding college student writing, widespread framings and re-framings of college student writing as rhetoric, composition, essay or theme writing, journalism, or something else, and as the province of first-year college students, underprepared students, or other categories of students. Many past versions of college student writing in America have already been captured in snapshots of teaching or learning practices at specific institutions, what I call site-specific histories of composition (e.g., Donahue and Moon; Ritter, *To Know, Before Shaughnessy*; Gold; Masters; Kates; Hobbs, *Nineteenth-Century*; L'Eplattenier and Mastrangelo; Varnum). Together, such histories along with increasingly nuanced understandings of past and present places of composition enable us to draw from multiple pasts. Also, they prepare us to consider the possibility that more than one history can emerge from the same institution and, grounded by different theoretical orientations to place, yield new insights.

It is the latter point, a multidimensional understanding of college student writing's past interactions with places, that I explore in this book. I argue that despite our type of institution or demographic surroundings, college student writing should be seen as an interaction between students and various overlapping and evolving places that were and are maintained through discourses, perceptions, social agreements, and physical resources. With this made visible, we move beyond concluding that writing is local or contextual (helpful though these points are) and beyond accumulating local histories, each a complication of what preceding histories have led us to expect about composition. In addition, we begin developing an analytical method that helps us untangle numerous *kinds* of figures and forces that have shaped, and may still shape, college student writing. The resulting perspective is never more needed than now, I believe, as we grapple with changes such as ever-diversifying student populations, pedagogical approaches that value multilingual and multimodal competencies, disciplinary growth, and intensified public and political scrutiny. In short, now, as our students and teaching methods change and as our commitments to educational stakeholders mature, we find ourselves in a fitting moment to both pluralize and specify what we mean when we associate college student writing with places beyond the classroom, with communities, ecologies, and publics.

Some of what's at stake appears in trends that are all too familiar to college faculty in America. In light of cuts in state funding to public colleges and universities, colleges and universities have had to strengthen their relationships to nearby civic and business groups. Given pressure to keep undergraduate English and writing studies majors competitive on the job market, English departments and writing programs have worked to secure internships and career counseling for their majors. Furthermore, given calls to broaden the purview of composition studies from "the" writing classroom to other sites and networks where writing occurs, evident, for example, in the Conference on College Composition and Communication's (CCCC) 2013 theme, "The Public Work of Composition," disciplinary attention has shifted from classroom-based writing to writing in workplaces and civic groups as well as to public dimensions of college writing. These and other developments suggest that we risk making college student writing anachronistic if we fail to discern how composition connects, sometimes conflictingly, to sites, organizations, and ideologies that thrive beyond campus borders.

To illustrate the perspective on writing that I explain in this book, I use two institutional cases from before the 1950s, when the CCCC established an annual tradition of organizing and managing writing instructors (Strickland), a tradition preceding composition's late-1960s status as a "social formation" (Zebroski 29). I look to the time before *composition* had become *Composition* because this period saw changes vivid enough to virtually demand analysis, changes capable of enriching our understanding of composition's spatial work in the past and present. Well-documented and widely felt academic developments in the late nineteenth century included a post-Civil War shift from rhetorical training grounded in memorizing and reciting classical rhetorical principles, studying political topics, and affecting a suitable tone when delivering speeches, to rhetorical training grounded in writing; a mid-1870s push, influenced by Harvard faculty and others, to use writing to test and sort incoming college students; a late-1880s tendency, supported by textbooks, to divide writing into the separate modes of narration, description, exposition, and argument; and the subsequent popularity of writing on observable topics (Connors; Kitzhaber; Brereton). By the early twentieth century, many faculty members at elite research universities evaluated student writing based on its adherence to textbook rules and grammar and punctuation conventions, though compelling alternative accounts continue to surface of female and other nontraditional college students writing with an eye toward social causes (e.g., Kates; Mastrangelo; Gold). And writing instruction in the 1940s is remembered for answering calls from the U.S. military to prioritize practical communication. However, lest these developments convey a tidy progression of events unrelated to other factors, we should acknowledge the overlap of various theories and social and economic changes. As Lisa Mastrangelo explains, identifying a single theory of writing instruction during the Progressive Era (1880-1920) is difficult because pragmatism preceded and coexisted with progressivism and early versions of feminism (xviii). Even Deweyian-Progressivism, which "focused on active and experiential learning" and "encouraged self-expression and the development of the individual," had roots in older philosophies (Mastrangelo 23). Also, looking at the 1930s-1940s, Cara A. Finnegan and Marissa Lowe Wallace argue that much of what we associate with World War II-era courses on practical communication could instead be located in Great Depression-era exigencies as college and university leaders worried about student retention (403). These and other scholars show that attempts to plot major developments of composition on a single timeline risk oversimplification.

Too, the study of English itself and the proliferation of academic departments in the late 1800s and early 1900s illustrate the degree of change surrounding composition before the 1950s. The mid nineteenth century saw a widespread rise of extracurricular and non-collegiate educational programs and sources, from the lyceum circuit to the national circulation of magazines, which rivaled college rhetoric coursework in influencing the public and, Thomas P. Miller argues, hastened the collegiate turn toward academic specialization (87). From the 1870s to the 1890s, classical and philosophical course sequences once seen as the core of a higher education expanded to include course sequences in science, commerce, and other types of specialization, such that by the early 1900s, faculty members who most championed specialization and research also demoted teaching (T. Miller 134-135). This portrayal echoes the research of Susan Miller and Sharon Crowley, who fault 1890s-era literary specialization for demoting writing and the teaching of writing in the university. Furthermore, as James A. Berlin argues, the late-nineteenth-century rise of specialization reflected broader social changes in that the American college "was to become an agent of upward social mobility" given new business and industry needs (60). Influenced by college-industry connections, America's college student population doubled in the decades around 1900 (Brereton 7). The number of women enrolling in colleges more than quadrupled from 1870 to 1890 and continued growing into the 1900s (Hobbs, "Introduction" 16), though as numerous historians have shown, perceptions of acceptable livelihoods for women lagged behind.

All this is to say nothing of changes to the mission and structure of American colleges and universities in the nineteenth and early twentieth centuries. In 1862, the U.S. government passed the Morrill Land-Grant Act, which supported the creation of universities focusing on agriculture and industry. Thus, many universities arose that now bear the designations "State" or "A&M," and the higher education landscape grew more crowded. In the 1870s, state normal schools, which trained teachers and which initially offered coursework leading to diplomas rather than college degrees, became a fixture in America's small and mid-sized cities. Over time, land-grant institutions and normal schools competed with older public and private postsecondary institutions so that by the late 1800s many institutions closed due to a lack of funds and students. By the 1910s many state normal schools became degree-granting normal colleges, and by the 1920s public junior colleges were founded in the hope of giving working students more affordable and accessible higher education options. Overlapping these developments was institutional restructuring evident from the late 1800s through the early 1900s as colleges and universities created new departments for faculty who narrowed their research interests and joined increasingly specific national organizations where the faculty could share their work with likeminded peers. So the Professor of Rhetoric and Belle Lettres in the early 1800s would have likely identified as Professor of Rhetoric and Mental and Moral Philosophy (or the like) in the mid 1800s, as Professor of Rhetoric and English Literature by 1900, and as Professor of Speech or as Professor of Literature by 1920. But one important factor persisted, albeit in multiple forms, throughout the many changes summarized above: students studied and practiced how to wield language effectively.

If looking before the late 1900s to a time when numerous groups vied to control student writing on college campuses (and a time period from which we now have some distance), I believe that we can examine competing interests within and beyond colleges that converged in composition courses and in other college writing initiatives, and we can enhance our view of the social, discursive, and physical places that affected college student writing. From this historical starting point, I extrapolate new ways to read today's interactions of college student writing with its surroundings. One of the institutional cases that I consider is college student writing at Ohio University (OU), a rural institution in the northern foothills of Appalachia and, given its 1804 founding, the oldest public university in the area now known as the Midwest. The other institutional case that I consider is college student writing at the University of Houston (UH), an urban institution founded in 1927 as a junior college in the south-central United States and in a metropolitan region that experienced explosive growth throughout the 1900s. These institutions are nearly opposites in terms of their origins, missions, student populations, and geographical locations. I select them for that reason as well as for the practical fact that I have taught and done historical research at both institutions, my time at each institution immersing me in some of the spatial issues discussed in the historical texts that they hold. While on site, I found surprising similarities in how the student writing at OU and at UH interacted with surrounding places and groups. Although separated by 1,200 miles and serving different communities, themes emerged from my research at these institutions, themes that the right theoretical perspective can make explicit and useable for researchers and teachers at other institutions.

Ohio University, frequently mistaken today for its larger, younger, and better-endowed peer The Ohio State University about seventy-five miles to the northwest, lies in the town of Athens, Athens County, in the southeastern part of the state and in the heart of the region now called Appalachian Ohio. Marked by hilly terrain, a small population, and a mining past, Appalachian Ohio, comprising the southeastern third of the state, is not what many people think of when they hear *Ohio*. Scholarly speakers who come to OU to attend conferences or other events usually fly in to the state capital of Columbus (home of The Ohio State University), a metropolitan region of nearly two million residents as of the 2010 U.S. Federal Census ("Annual Estimates"). Then the speakers take an hour-and-a-half road trip from the flat lands of central Ohio to the hilly and more sparsely populated lands to the southeast, in effect entering a new social and physiographic region. The trees multiply, the roads begin winding, the speed limit decreases, and the towns shrink. During my years at OU, I overheard more than one visiting scholar remark that the drive from Columbus to Athens made them wonder whether they were lost and should expect to end up in West Virginia.

However, for all of the signs of remoteness that the drive from Columbus to Athens brings today, events from Ohio's early history reveal a more complex picture of the state's center and margins. First, Ohio, as it is known today, was not settled all at once but in pieces, the product of multiple purchases made by an investment group called the Ohio Company of Associates. The Ohio Company focused initially on land near the Ohio River, now along the border of Ohio and West Virginia, and then worked westward and northward. Second, according to Thomas Nathaniel Hoover, twentieth-century OU faculty member and historian, when OU co-founder Manasseh Cutler interacted with members of Congress in the late 1700s, Cutler demanded "lands for a university not at the center of the [Ohio Company of Associates'] *entire* purchase but at the center of the *first* 1,500,000 acres" (T. Hoover 10, emphasis added). So as of 1799, the Ohio town now known as Athens was called *Middletown* to signify its location in the middle of the Ohio Company's first purchase of land west of the Ohio River (T. Hoover 21). Third, among the first names considered by Manasseh Cutler for a university in this newly acquired region were American University and then, in conjunction with other planners, American Western University, names suggesting a great deal about the ideals attached to this institution during westward-oriented nation building. Founded among these lofty sentiments, Middletown soon became Athens, and American Western University, lying in what had temporarily been the middle of a new settlement, soon found itself demoted to the name *Ohio University* and occupying land in the southeastern corner of a western- and northern-expanding economic and political entity. Visitors to OU today who wonder why the university is located where it is find much to consider upon realizing that Ohio's southeastern border was once seen as a center.

Enrolling no more than a couple of hundred students at a time throughout the 1800s, any changes to OU's white male student population were conspicuous. The institution enrolled its first male African American student in 1824; in 1828, the student became the first African American to graduate from college in all of the Midwest. Women of all racial backgrounds were slower to join the student body, the first female student enrolling in 1868 in the preparatory department, at which time she used (or was given) a gender-anonymous version of her name in the university catalog (*Ohio University Bulletin, 1868-1869* 11). She graduated in 1873, revealing OU's rather late attempts to support coeducation compared to Oberlin College, which had transitioned to a coed student population in the 1830s and 1840s. Female African American students followed, beginning in the 1870s. Finally, the early twentieth century saw greater geographical diversity among OU students, namely a rise in students from all over Ohio as opposed to a population comprised primarily of students from southeastern Ohio counties; and OU admitted at least one international student as early as 1895.

The University of Houston's history is as or more intertwined in spatial and other transformations. It was founded and initially governed by the Houston Independent School District (HISD) in 1927 as Houston Junior College (HJC), half of a pair of racially segregated junior colleges: HJC, attended by white students, and Houston Colored Junior College (HCJC), attended by African American students. Unlike at OU in the nineteenth century, these colleges taught male and female students from their beginnings. Also, the timing and state location of the junior colleges' foundings fit national trends, for 1927 has been called "the peak year for new junior colleges" (Witt et al. 44), and in the late 1920s, Texas trailed only California in the founding of new public junior colleges (Witt et al. 51). The city of Houston's growth was equally remarkable at the time: by 1920 it boasted 138,276 residents, and by 1930 it had become the largest city in Texas, with 292,352 residents ("Historical Population"). Subsequent decades continued to see significant population growth given the normalization of technological advances such as highways and air-conditioning. Amid local and national developments, HJC and HCJC served as Houston's first public postsecondary institutions, though it would be many more years before these institutions became self-governing. As of 1928, the one-year-old HJC, with 510 students and 25 faculty members, called itself "the largest junior college in Texas" (Cochran 51-52), yet both HJC and HCJC lacked campuses of their own, as did most public junior colleges in Texas at that time (Witt et al. 55) and many of the earliest public junior colleges across the country (Beach 5). Houston's HJC and HCJC held their classes in the evenings at public high schools, HJC at San Jacinto High School in the centrally located neighborhood now called Midtown and HCJC at Jack Yates High School in the Third Ward, a primarily African American neighborhood on the city's east side. When the need arose, city churches also provided room for the colleges' class meetings. So initially, HJC and HCJC operated as educational concepts that were put into practice in borrowed rooms and buildings—concepts whose visible reality manifested when students gathered at approved locations to learn.

The 1930s and 1940s saw significant developments for HJC and HCJC, from the adoption of permanent campuses, to changes in institutional category as the junior colleges, which had been governed by the HISD, became independent state-supported universities offering graduate and undergraduate programs. Key moments of change follow:

- 1934: HJC became the University of Houston (UH), and HCJC became the Houston College for Negroes (HCN). This marked a shift in emphasis from two-year course tracks to four-year course tracks.
- 1939: UH moved to its permanent campus where it could offer day classes freely as well as graduate classes.
- 1945: UH became a self-governing private institution as opposed to an HISD-governed institution.
- 1946: HCN moved to its permanent campus, separated by a few city blocks from the UH campus.
- 1947: HCN became the Texas State University for Negroes (later shortened to Texas State University), an independent state-supported institution.

Initially funded by the Houston Public School Board and supervised by the HISD, the earliest versions of the University of Houston and Texas Southern University moved, physically and politically, toward independence between 1927 and 1950. Given my employment at and familiarity with UH, I focus most of my Houston-based research on its institutional holdings; however, in Chapter Three, I also consider 1930s-era essays written by HCN seniors because these essays give perspectives from African American students whose college education was controlled by the HISD.

OU's centuries-old history is one of slow transformation from center to margins, and UH's shorter history is one of fast-rising prominence and visibility. Indeed, the latter institution's history is shaped by a search for an identity within and beyond Houston as the city grew outward in all directions and as residents tried to discern what it meant to constitute Texas's largest city. In demographic trends as in related economic and cultural trends, the cases of OU and UH are opposites; doubtlessly, other colleges and universities in America have found themselves somewhere between the two pictures that I am painting as populations move, enrollments change, and institutional significance shifts. Exceedingly rare is the institution that avoids change.

RETHINKING PLACE AND HISTORY

Place and history, the concepts at the heart of this project, are by now familiar in Rhetoric and Composition; and to a great extent, my work builds on disciplinary movements from the last twenty years that have situated composition in an array of richly described locations and expanded composition history to include previously unrecognized sites and voices. However, I maintain that the very popularity of movements to localize college student writing and pluralize historical narratives of college student writing has created a need for scholars to look more deliberately and carefully than they are used to doing at how they *place* student writing.

Scholarly work on place transcends a single theoretical lineage, research method, or political goal. Whether we produce knowledge from the angle of place-based education (Gruenewald and Smith), a trialectics of space (Soja; Grego and Thompson), spatial rhetorics (Enoch, "Finding"), or critical regionalism (Powell); whether we write ethnographies, conduct surveys or interviews, or analyze texts; and whether we do research with the hope of shaping a new social, political, economic, or physical landscape, we follow paths already trod by scholars who have examined place. Rhetoric and Composition's ecological turn, stemming from work by Marilyn Cooper, Margaret A. Syverson, and Richard Coe, led in 2001 to the pedagogical theory known as ecocomposition (Weisser and Dobrin, *Ecocomposition*), one of the field's most obvious twenty-first-century manifestations of spatial thinking. In *Ecocomposition: Theoretical and Pedagogical Approaches* (2001), editors Christian R. Weisser and Sidney I. Dobrin view writing as a practice of creating or sustaining links among people, things, and ideas. It is, they say, about "relationships; it is about the coconstitutive existence of writing and environment; it is about physical environment and constructed environment; it is about the production of written discourse and the relationship of that discourse to the places it encounters" ("Breaking" 2). Outside of ecocomposition, scholars have taken up ecological theories to describe rhetorical phenomena (Goggin; Rice; Fleckenstein et al.; Rivers and Weber; Devet), sometimes to inform teaching practices, while other scholars have used cultural and feminist geography to advance knowledge about how, and with what consequences, writing is a social act (e.g., Reynolds). At the same time, postmodern ideas from the likes of Richard Rorty and Edward Soja have crossed scholarly fields and supported analyses of writers whose members interact according to rules established by particular communities or societies. Additionally, place-conscious education (Gruenewald and Smith; Brooke), by striving to create sustainable physical environments, has provided another, more empirical view of place. From those of us who identify primarily as instructors to those of us who identify primarily as researchers or scholars, and everyone in between (e.g., teacher-researchers at National Writing Project sites), seeing writing through ever more considerations of place has given us options for moving beyond the acknowledgement that writing is a social or cultural act. Due to the sheer amount and range of scholarship on place, it is now not only helpful but also, I believe, crucial for us to specify what we mean when we discuss places of writing or rhetoric.

The central challenge for people in Rhetoric and Composition who study place is quickly becoming a challenge of specificity, of spelling out what exact conception of place we mean and how we can study places of writing without attempting to study everything: all discourses, any number of social groups, numerous intersecting physical sites. While of course we can return to ethnographic analyses of ways that selected populations use texts, as in Shirley Brice Heath's famous *Ways with Words* (1983), recent contributions from ecological theories, critical regionalism, and so on demand that scholars account for more of the messiness of the practice and effects of situated writing. We must heed questions such as, how should we decide which contexts of writing to study and why? And: what do we miss if we strive to isolate a classroom of student writers for study apart from related sociopolitical contexts?

Also noteworthy in recent decades is the proliferation of histories of composition, providing pictures of pre-1950s college writing and writing pedagogy at institutions that have only recently been seen as worthy of notice: normal schools, rural institutions, historically Black colleges and universities (HBCUs), women's colleges, and institutions populated by working-class and/or non-white-majority students. Now, in addition to realizing that how we teach writing has been shaped by attitudes from late-nineteenth-century teachers at Harvard who valued grammatical correctness and thematic unity (Kitzhaber; Brereton; Connors), we have begun to see other, underexplored genealogies in our occupational family tree. Some of the many contributions in this area include Lucille M. Schultz's *The Young Composers: Composition's Beginnings in Nineteenth-Century Schools*, which exposes influences on colleges and universities from assignments at common schools; Kelly Ritter's *Before Shaughnessy: Basic Writing at Yale and Harvard, 1920-1960*, which uses hitherto marginalized remedial writing programs at Yale and Harvard to argue for site-specific developmental writing instruction; David Gold's *Rhetoric in the Margins: Revising the History of Writing Instruction in American Colleges, 1873-1947*, which shows how certain Southern, African American, female, and working-class institutions merged conservative teaching methods and progressive goals; and Patricia Donahue and Gretchen Flesher Moon's edited collection, *Local Histories: Reading the Archives of Composition*, which features site-specific portrayals of composition as influenced by occupational divisions, social classes, and individual instructors.

The usual goal of local histories of composition—to offer examples, descriptions, or stories that give recognition where it is due and complicate previous grand narratives—is one that I support even though it is not my primary goal here. Such a goal goes back at least to 1995 when the contributors to Catherine Hobbs' *Nineteenth-Century Women Learn to Write* used thick description, of sorts, to expose under recognized social tensions navigated by early female college students at particular Northeastern and Midwestern institutions. The goal persisted when, over a decade later, Gold showed how, and with effects, faculty members at three little-known Texas institutions mixed ideologies and teaching practices, and when Donahue and Moon's contributors shared information about individual instructors and students who overcame obstacles amid trying learning environments. Despite the fact that readers can learn from the site-specific examples that such histories provide (e.g., Masters; Ritter, *To Know*, *Before Shaughnessy*; Enoch, *Refiguring*; Kates; Varnum), I don't want to ask readers who teach at other postsecondary institutions to remember and retrieve details from an ever-growing body of research on individual colleges and universities. As this research grows, so do readers' challenges in plucking insights from it. It doesn't take long before readers of local histories of composition ask: which local examples best guide the writing assignments that I assign and the relationships that I cultivate? Should I stick to examples from my current region and examples that reflect my institution's history or academic classification? Perhaps foreseeing this difficulty, David Gold poses the following question after he describes the teaching and philosophy of Melvin Tolson, an African American professor at Wiley College in east Texas: "Is it possible for a white professor to participate in the traditional role of the black HBCU professor as an interpreter of the cultural experience (Roebuck and Murty 118) for her black students?" (Gold 62). Gold responds by suggesting that readers embrace "the contradictions in our teaching" (ibid). But if one compares the case of Wiley College to other, equally compelling historical cases of teaching or learning, a question remains: which examples of teaching and learning—which local histories—should the reader draw from and why?

The challenge for the potential user of local histories of composition is to sift through and evaluate the great range of cases before her based on her location and needs. After all, creators of local histories have long defended their work for its ability to enlarge the pedagogical repertoire of the liberally minded scholar, instructor, or writing program administrator (WPA). For example, in *Practicing Writing: The Postwar Discourse of Freshman English*, Thomas M. Masters supports Richard Miller's goal of giving current WPAs "tolerance for ambiguity, an appreciation for structured contradictions, a perspicuity that draws into its purview the multiple forces determining individual events and actions," among other assets (qtd. in Masters 26). Other historians flesh out and defend perspectives from under recognized student or faculty populations (Ritter, *To Know* 6, *Before Shaughnessy* 9; Moon 4-5; Gold x), as do historians who emphasize rhetoric over composition (Enoch, *Refiguring* 10-11; Kates 1; Bordelon 4). As informative as this work is, its very range, like the range of research on place, pushes readers to ask: how will I determine how to navigate the local cases before me? How will I decide which cases to draw from for inspiration or practical guidance, and when?

Chapter One

The two movements that I am discussing, one to situate present-day writing through notions of place, the other to localize historical student writing, have developed at roughly the same time but without one movement seriously engaging the other. Local histories continue to offer detailed narratives of occurrences at newly studied colleges or universities albeit without always theorizing the places that they describe—their descriptions often substituting for spatial analysis. Meanwhile, theories of place continue to proliferate, yet without substantial application to histories of college student writing. I would like to change this, and in effect, to theorize place through historical studies of college student writing. So in the remainder of this book, I proceed a little differently from past historians of composition: I shift attention from historical site-specific examples, descriptions, or stories themselves to *kinds of interactions* suggested by historical site-specific details. The shift recalls Stephen Toulmin's ethical system for privileging "types of cases and situations" over general laws about humankind on the one hand and over particular examples of human activity on the other hand (107). Though elsewhere I refrain from referencing law or ethics, I make a similar move as Toulmin—toward sharing a few *kinds* of interactions between student writing at specific institutions and other forces, kinds of interaction that are supported by historical sources from more than one university. My goal is to present some lines of analysis that readers can take, amend if they so desire, and apply to institutions other than those that I consider here. In addition to showing diversity in teaching practices and learning goals, I focus on giving composition instructors and scholars takeaways to apply to their own teaching locations in the past or present. That is, I want to help composition instructors and scholars think through how student writing at various institutions, including but not limited to the institutions where the instructors teach, moves through glocal webs and yields transferable insights about writing (and the teaching of writing) as a contextually multidimensional act.

One point of emphasis from ecological theories that is relevant to my study is the situating of writing in multiple and sometimes messy contexts. For example, consider Kristie S. Fleckenstein et al.'s call for research on contextually rich writing:

> To flourish, writing studies must generate individual research projects that focus on a wide array of contexts, from the bodies of individual writers to classrooms, workplaces, clubs, churches, neighborhoods, virtual environments, and historical moments. This aspect of diversity impels researchers to seek out different contexts for writing, to read beyond their normal scope of disciplinary literature, and to redraw the circumfer-

ence of immersion. (401)

I share Fleckenstein et al.'s embrace of multiple contexts, but I fear that, like much recent theorizing about place, this approach fails to resolve a problem of focus. Histories of composition that examine a breadth of contexts can quickly become unwieldy unless the researcher makes tough and principled choices about which contexts to study and where to place parameters around a research project. Key research concerns become, which strands in ever-enlarging glocal webs of people, ideas, and places should one select to study? How does one keep from studying how composition has related to everything, from local demographics to the widespread dissemination of tools such as pencils? So to give shape to my analysis of historical student writing, I organize my study of pre-1950s student writing at OU and UH around a few concepts that have long informed—we might say, situated—the study of rhetoric: concepts from sophistic and neosophistic perspectives on language. The concepts that I summarize below orient readers to specific ways that language, in this case college student writing, has interacted and may still interact with its surroundings.

STUDY: THEORY AND SCOPE

The late twentieth century saw a revival and modernizing of First Sophistic teachings on the part of scholars in Communication Studies and then, by the 1980s and 1990s, from scholars in Rhetoric and Composition. As the latter's social turn revealed expansive new ways to study writing, questions and concerns from the First Sophists gained renewed attention, and Rhetoric and Composition scholars such as Sharon Crowley, Susan C. Jarratt, Victor J. Vitanza, Bruce McComiskey, and Ken Lindblom came to treat language as always perspectival, interested, and situated—always partial tellings of a subject and contingent on the purposes of a rhetor or rhetors. It is not my wish to review this disciplinary movement in full. Given the recurrence and complexity of debates about how First Sophistic ideas can be understood by contemporary scholars, a debate involving mainly Vitanza and Communication Studies scholars John Poulakos and Edward Schiappa and reaching back to historiographical concepts from Richard Rorty, such a review could comprise a book of its own. Suffice it to say that I endorse John Poulakos' work to update terms and issues that were important to ancient teachers associated with sophistic outlooks, and I support the category *neosophistic rhetorical theory* to account for scholars who use and modernize ideas from ancient sophists for contemporary communication contexts, as I do here.

Edward Schiappa defines "neo-sophistic rhetorical theory and criticism" as "efforts to draw on sophistic thinking in order to contribute to contemporary theory and practice," and he places the work of rhetorical theorists Michael C. Leff and Susan C. Jarratt in this category ("Neo-Sophistic" 195). It bears mentioning that this definition does not render neosophistic rhetorical theory synonymous with Richard Rorty's better-known historiographical category of rational reconstruction even though the two overlap. Rational reconstruction is largely a one-way street, the use of present-day understandings to make new sense of the past. Neosophistic rhetorical theory, however, is more specific, necessarily inspired by early sophistic teachings, and this theoretical approach contains an important extra step: it "… concerns the appropriation of certain sophistic doctrines insofar as they contribute solutions to contemporary problems" (McComiskey, "Neo-Sophistic Rhetorical" 17; see also McComiskey, *Gorgias*). So neosophistic rhetorical theory 1) starts from the modern-day researcher's perspective; 2) allows the researcher to take insights gained from, or at least inspired by, early sophistic teachings (material from the past); and 3) encourages the researcher to see how that information informs modern-day practices. It is not just the present making sense of the past (rational reconstruction), but the present using aspects of the past to understand the present anew. Susan C. Jarratt, in "Toward a Sophistic Historiography," shows how such a definition can be put into practice. She uses sophistic principles to advocate studies of texts across modern-day disciplines, explore implications of knowledge gaps, and tie texts to social conventions that decide, at any given moment, which persuasive strategies a society finds convincing and which communication goals a society deems valuable ("Toward"). Most relevant for my project is Jarratt's urging for scholars to tolerate contradictions across historical narratives and for scholars to prioritize probability and multiple narratives over a sense of historical singularity—even if one narrative has long been accepted as reliable ("Toward" 272). Beyond building on ancient sophistic ideas to re-see the present, Jarratt reminds us of the need to treat whatever new understandings and narratives we create as provisional, tied to the kind of sources, people, and situations at hand.

From the recent mining of First Sophistic teachings for contemporary purposes, that is, from neosophistic rhetorical theory, I take a few concepts that highlight specific analytical threads available to the researcher who sees knowledge and language as situated and political. I take this step even as I recognize that since the 1990s, many sophistic concepts (e.g., *kairos*) have mainstreamed into rhetorical studies generally, while other sophistic concepts (e.g., *dynaton*) have faded from view. Soon after Edward Schiappa criticized late-twentieth-century scholars for taking ancient ideas from individual sophists and thereafter constructing a sophistic rhetorical tradition ("Neo-Sophistic," "Sophistic Rhetoric"), scholars in Rhetoric and Composition, with some exceptions (Vitanza, *Writing Histories*, *Negation*; Greenbaum), moved away from calling their work sophistic and instead began to call their work ecological, feminist, or geographical. (Notably, Vitanza advances his Third Sophistic project in the service of historiography and of a broad view of Western rhetoric, not in reference to local histories of college writing.) By 2010 when *Composition Forum* published an interview with Susan C. Jarratt titled "Still Sophistic (After All These Years)" (Holiday), one's use of *sophistic* made a strong statement about the continued value of underscoring a non-foundational pre-Aristotelian intellectual heritage. I, too, would like to make a statement by organizing my historical analyses through concepts that I trace to the early sophists. With this approach, I argue that despite whether Rhetoric and Composition scholars now use sophistic terminology regularly, many of our assumptions about language remain indebted to pre-Aristotelian sophistic thinking, especially that of fourth-century BCE sophist Gorgias of Leontini, who practiced a "time- and place-specific" logic (Poulakos, "The Logic" 13). Above all, I argue that those of us interested in contexts of writing and histories of college student writing can sharpen our analytical vision by foregrounding sophistic concepts that have fallen into relative disuse as well as sophistic concepts that have mainstreamed quickly, leaving their critical potential underappreciated.

Although when I began studying pre-1950s students writing at OU and UH I felt tempted to organize my research through thick description or imaginative narratives, or by presenting historical information with minimal commentary (Ritter, "Archival"; Brereton), I realized that in order to account for the spatial complexity that I sensed but couldn't quite articulate and unpack, I needed other analytical tools. Inspired in particular by Poulakos' explanation of three concepts that showed an outlook shared by multiple sophists (*Sophistical*), I organized my account of the relationships between student writing at OU and UH and other forces via the concepts of *nomos*, *kairos*, *epideixis*, and *dynaton*. (See the Glossary for concise definitions of these terms as well as some terms important in the history of American higher education.) So guided, I tracked connections between student writing at these universities and influences (mostly, people and ideas) within and beyond campus borders. My findings showed that shapers of composition practices included savvy instructors, administrators, and students (people usually highlighted in studies of historical student writing), as well as civic clubs, city leaders, physical infrastructure, state politicians, and K-12 and other postsecondary education organizations (people and entities usually considered in histories of literacy or community rhetoric, such as Royster and Gere). My analysis shows how such forces and groups intermingled, frequently in a close geographical area, with the result of constructing a certain kind of public university, student population, and writing environment. At OU and UH, "college" student writing belonged as much to a bevy of surrounding people and

Chapter One

interests as it did to students—a perspective worth applying to student writing today. From this angle, boundaries blur between the concepts of college and community, composition and rhetoric, education and politics, and local and regional, and even among the categories of students, teachers, administrators, and community members; and a picture begins to emerge about what it can look like for researchers and teachers to make new knowledge from and about places of writing.

Each of the four concepts that guides my analysis bears a sophistic lineage that evolved in the hands of post-First Sophistic thinkers from Aristotle to contemporary theorists, yet each concept nonetheless retains ties to earlier sophistic outlooks. While for explanatory purposes I focus on one concept at a time, the concepts work synergistically by steadily familiarizing us with the work of rethinking who and what is involved when college students write. Also, the four concepts comprise some of many other ways of seeing, a few starting points among others that await articulation. The first of the concepts that I consider, *nomos* (plural *nomoi*), was used by the fifth-century BCE sophist Antiphon, among others, to refer to social rules or conventions. In fragments that remain from his treatise *On Truth*, Antiphon examines nomos by comparing it to *physis*, or nature: people determine nomos while the gods determine physis. Classics scholar Michael Gagarin elaborates by pointing out that for Antiphon, *physis* entailed features like breathing that everyone shares regardless of their societal affiliation (Gagarin 66-67). From this perspective, nomos supplements physis by "impos[ing] rules on matters that *physis* leaves unregulated" (Gagarin 69). But whereas Antiphon's attitude toward nomos was ambiguous, other sophists embraced the concept's usefulness—Gorgias in his popular *Encomium of Helen* and *Defense of Behalf of Palamedes*. For neosophistic rhetorical theorists, the most intriguing and useful aspects of nomos include its suggestion of the mutability of social rules (McComiskey 33) and its implication that discourse itself is connected to political interests (Jarratt, *Rereading* 74). As Jarratt puts it, "though normally applied to law, by implication [nomos] could be taken to deny the possibility of any discourse—'literary' or 'philosophic,' for example—isolated from the operation of social customs and political power" (*Rereading* 74). Importantly for my purposes in Chapter Two, Jarratt adds that the "provisional codes (habits or customs) of social and political behavior" designated by *nomos* are geographically specific (ibid). So as I examine specific institutional sites where pre-1950s student writing at OU and UH trafficked, I ask, what nomoi shaped the writing? And I suggest nomoi that we should heed today.

The second concept with sophistic roots that I use, because it complements and complicates a perspective from the angle of nomos, is kairos. Before the early sophists, kairos referred to ideas such as "due measure" and "proportion"

(Schiappa, *Protagoras* 73). Through its handling by the sophists, kairos came to mean the timeliness of a message, that is, the utterance of a message suitably near in time to the event or message to which it responds. We see the concept referring to timeliness in the anonymously authored text *Dissoi Logoi* and in the contributions of Gorgias. But for Gorgias as well as his student Alcidamas, kairotic action was not defined by timeliness alone; it could also signal a departure from expected communication in favor of inventive extemporaneous speech (Tindale 117; E. White 14; Poulakos, *Sophistical* 61; see also McComiskey 112). The fact that the meaning of kairos continues to grow should not trouble us, I believe, and in Chapter Three I follow Bruce McComiskey's contemporary updating of kairos so that it primarily emphasizes the feature of responsiveness, whether sudden or planned. The resulting easing of temporal constraints suits a study of writing as opposed to speech, and it allows consideration of questions such as, to whom or what was student writing responding, whether directly, as in the form of work completed for academic credit, or indirectly, as in work that countered perceptions and opinions from elsewhere? Whereas nomos focuses attention on behavioral codes that student writers uphold or try to change, my use of kairos shifts attention to textual conversations involving both college student writing and discourses from a surrounding state or city.

The remaining two concepts that I take from the rehabilitation of First Sophistic teachings are *epideixis* (plural *epideixeis*), as in the now familiar category epideictic rhetoric, and dynaton. A popular definition of epideictic rhetoric is ornate language used in ceremonial occasions to praise or blame, language fitting to contribute to a spectacle. But it is important to add that before Aristotle codified this term in his *Rhetoric*, epideixis concerned language that displayed one's rhetorical prowess to an audience as opposed to language that achieved practical or private purposes (McComiskey 90; see also Kerferd 28). That is, for many of the sophists who preceded Aristotle, epideictic language could be used primarily to impress by showing one's facility with words. Accounts of early sophists' epideictic speeches reach us through Socratic dialogues including *Gorgias*, *Hippias Major*, *Protagorus*, *Axiochus*, and *Eryxias*, as well as through the work of Thucydides (Guthrie 41-42), among other sources, so in many cases non-sophists used *epideixis* to describe the work of early sophists. We can detect something of an epideictic effect in the early sophists' language by turning to Protagoras of Abdera, who reportedly said that teaching, education, and wisdom are "the garland of fame which is woven from the flowers of an eloquent tongue and set on the heads of those who love it." In addition to bringing fame, he continued, an eloquent tongue's "flowers" lead applauding audiences and teachers to "rejoice" ("Graeco-Syrian" 127). Heighted and poetic language of this kind displayed one's learning and thus enhanced one's reputation. Also, such discursive moves reflected early theatrical language, which privileged "show, appearance, art, deception, imitation, illusion, and entertainment" (Poulakos, *Sophistical* 41). So when early sophists applied these features to non-theatrical discourses, the sophists highlighted the discursive construction of reality in various venues (Poulakos, *Sophistical* 39; Consigny 284). And as early sophists took theatrical language beyond the realm of theater, the sophists produced what Bruce McComiskey calls "a new amalgam—the amalgam that Aristotle would later call epideictic rhetoric" (McComiskey 43). In my application of this tradition to historical student writing at OU and UH, I ask, what relationships were evident between historical student writing and occasions for displaying the writing openly? How did the opportunity to *exhibit* student writing affect the writing's effect? From such questions, I consider occasions today when faculty, administrators and others hold up student writing for public acclaim.

Finally, adding another dimension to my analysis is the idea of *to dynaton*, or *to dunaton*, which I will refer to here simply as *dynaton*. Like epideixis, dynaton was codified by Aristotle, but the concept first appeared sometime earlier. In his translation of Aristotle's *Metaphysics, Book IX*, Montgomery Furth associates dynaton with the terms "potent, potential, able, capable, possible" (qtd. in Aristotle 132), adding that context shapes the exact translation. However, most neosophistic rhetorical theorists approximate dynaton's meaning with the English word *possibility*. We find dynaton appearing in Plato's *Theaetetus* and *Gorgias*, though its availability as a descriptor of many sophists' ideas comes from John Poulakos, who explains the cultural context surrounding the work of selected ancient sophists. In his view, dynaton kept speakers mindful of the fact that "what is actual [i.e., agreed upon as factual] has not always been so but has resulted from a sequence of possibles" (*Sophistical* 69). Stressing the concept's emphasis on novel ways of thinking and acting, Poulakos adds, "If the orator's display succeeds in firing the imagination of the listeners, and if their hopes triumph over their experience of the world as it is, the possibilities before them are well on their way to becoming actuality" (ibid). So, too, I argue, concerning composition historiography, or how we study historical student writing. I use the concept of dynaton to inform an analysis of people involved in early-twentieth-century composition at OU and UH who crossed boundaries between local and global contexts and between academic and professional spheres. Comparing and contrasting the movements made by these people at OU and UH, I re-present local histories of composition as comparisons of *movements or changes* rather than as snapshots of familiar and clearly bounded scenes of writing such as writing from Illinois, writing from women's colleges, or writing from underprepared students. I argue that beyond geographical location and demographic facts, historical student writing in the past and present can be understood through its associations with variously identifying people and with variously situated ideas, and the work of tracing these associations can expand our sense of what composition is.

Herein lies the primary contribution of my project. Although I am invested in the work of localizing student writing and I champion site-based particularity, my analyses of historical student writing at OU and UH resist the overarching goal of accumulating site-specific historical information to fill gaps in previous narratives of composition history. Instead, my analyses use site-specific historical information to expose *kinds* of interactions that exist in different forms across colleges and universities. We are missing the boat, I suggest, if we see student writing today as unrelated to kinds of interactions that shaped the writing in Composition's pre-disciplinary history and if we sidestep opportunities to apply our rhetorically informed method of interpreting site-specific insights to other colleges and universities. Those of us studying composition's past via a particular college or university can build on transferable ways of seeing how college student writing relates to glocal factors trafficking in shifting social and discursive (and physical) terrain. Scholars and instructors with this perspective stand to resituate composition many times over, each time noticing new interactions between the work that goes on in the classroom and the work that goes on throughout campus or beyond campus borders. Students stand to learn what it means that writing assignments and activities come from multiple somewheres, filtered through regional and institutional needs, tied to institutional leaders' goals, and bearing influences from people who traverse or have traversed composition classes: those instructors who specialize in something other than Rhetoric and Composition, guest speakers who are brought to composition classes, people with whom instructors of all stripes associate at conferences and community events, people with whom instructors associated before teaching or researching composition. Finally, those instructors who study historical composition texts at their place of work stand to see how, even if their immediate teaching environments differ from teaching environments found at other colleges and universities, they can adapt insights from other locally focused historians.

Chapters Two through Five each uses a sophistic concept to analyze the local or glocal meaning of a set of historical texts at rural nineteenth-century-founded Ohio University and urban twentieth-century-founded University of Houston. Following Jarratt ("Toward" 272), each chapter brings up factors that allow the historical narrative presented to complement and occasionally contradict the historical narratives presented by surrounding chapters. Also, each chapter exposes ways that student writing at OU and UH, despite obvious institutional differences, experienced similar kinds of relationships to its surroundings. Chapter Two, which centralizes nomos, considers an 1870s diary and a 1920s scrapbook in the case of OU and 1920s-1930s student newspaper articles in the case of UH. These texts were selected because each contains detailed observations and opinions from students about student behavior at their university (a point that I connect to nomos). Chapter Three, drawing on kairos, considers late-1800s literary society records, student newspapers, and creative writing in the case of OU and a combination of 1920s-1930s student newspaper articles and 1930s senior papers, which functioned like undergraduate theses, in the cases of UH and the Houston College for Negroes. These texts were selected because they brought up sociopolitical contexts surrounding the university, contexts in which the university formed or grew (a point that I connect to a writing-focused version of kairos). Chapter Four, focusing on epideictic communication, considers a three-volume student-written history of OU in the case of that institution and issues from 1936 to 1950 of the student-written magazine *The Harvest* in the case of UH. These texts were chosen because they provide examples of student writing that was taken from classroom contexts and made into a display of student achievement for audiences other than students. Chapter Five, using dynaton to organize its findings, rethinks common ways of organizing local histories of composition by examining how people and ideas at OU and UH have moved through composition classes while bearing traces of their past involvements in social, professional, and disciplinary networks. This chapter relies on an array of source types, from local and national newspapers to biographies, yearbooks, and course catalogs, to illustrate ways that numerous influences wove through historical composition courses.

Most of the primary sources that I cite from Chapters Two through Five come from the archives at OU and UH: Ohio University's Robert E. and Jean R. Mahn Center for Archives and Special Collections housed in Alden Library, Athens, Ohio, and the University of Houston's Special Collections housed in M.D. Anderson Library, Houston, Texas. However, the boundaries of these and other archives grow fainter each year as collections are digitized, sometimes with the help of other organizations (e.g., the Ohio Historical Society), and as sources are retained in multiple forms and places: bound volumes as well as microfilm, books kept in officially designated archives as well as books kept in a library's annex or general holdings. Therefore, when I call the bulk of my research *archival*, I mean that most of the historical sources that I studied are held in some form in the archives that I named above. The sources may also be held elsewhere, and some source types, such as major historical newspapers, may be retrieved through a library's general databases. As archived materials continue to reach more readers and viewers who cannot travel to a particular collection, I ask that readers place generous conceptual parameters around the term *archive*. Building on Linda Ferreira-Buckley's work, Gesa E. Kirsch and Liz Rohan argue for "an expanded conception of archives" involving "our family, social, and cultural history" as well as traditional historical texts ("Introduction" 3). Although I do not follow their advice fully, I sympathize with their point: historical texts may have value despite their designation as archival. So, occasionally, I consider historical sources that speak back in provocative ways to my main archived sources—for example, using documents from an early Houston women's club that show why the club funded the studies of certain early UH students.

Chapter Six concludes my project by explaining how each of the analyses from the previous chapters unsettles common understandings of *local* writing and how each of the analyses complicates traditional understandings of *composition*, *literacy*, and *rhetoric*. None of these concepts alone is adequate, the chapter maintains. Finally, the chapter discusses ways that instructors at various colleges and institutions may use the analyses that I have illustrated to shape how they orient their students to writing and place. Despite whether instructors and scholars work at the institutions that I studied for this project, or at institutions in the same region or institutions that are similar in type to the institutions that I studied, instructors and scholars can rethink the analytical threads that I share based on the historical texts available to them and the issues that they find most pressing in the locations where they teach.

Above all, *Placing the History of College Writing: Stories from the Incomplete Archive* is intended to help readers interested in applying historical knowledge about composition as well as rhetoric to college student writing and the teaching of writing at their institutions; in the process, I hope that the book helps these readers reconceptualize what *composition* can mean, what individual, programmatic, institutional, communal, or regional visions it promotes and what opportunities for agency it creates. Also, as the book's subtitle suggests, it is intended to help those whose access to traditional sources of composition history (see Masters 2; Brereton xv-xvi) is limited by the sources kept by their institution, sources that, if judged based on the standards of previous histories of composition, might seem unrelated to composition or so distant from composition as to be useless. Many researchers would hesitate before studying composition history via students' yearbooks, newspaper articles, or creative pieces, or before studying composition history by looking at funding and programming from civic clubs. Such judgments of historical sources and interpretive options do not necessarily hold, I argue, because almost any college or university archive holds texts that speak to the context of one's institution. What matters, then, is figuring out how to make sense of context (or of place) in a way that helps researchers at more than one site—a task that, without clear organizational guideposts, risks being as vague and unhelpful as accounts of *nature* or *society*. If properly focused, the act of situating student writing in relation to place(s) can help historians and instructors revise their outlooks and their teaching.

CHAPTER TWO
CUSTOMIZING COMPOSITION: STUDENTS BROADENING BEHAVIORAL CODES

One revealing and previously undervalued way that historical student writing has related to people and ideas is through the writing's ties to institutional, or site-specific, expectations for student behavior. In question form, this relationship might be expressed as: to what extent did student writing do the work of upholding rules about how students should act and what students should prioritize at their university? The answer tells us one kind of story about the rhetorical work of student writing, a story of students using their writing to maintain or revise the roles granted them by their higher education institutions.

In a general sense, studying historical student writing in relation to a people's customs, as opposed to a people's specialized body of knowledge, is an old analytical move. It formed part of the thesis of *Composition-Rhetoric: Backgrounds, Theory, and Pedagogy*, in which Robert J. Connors portrayed late-nineteenth-century composition in American colleges as an answer to social needs (7-8). Since Connors' book, many scholars have gestured to the role of institutional customs in contributing to historical student writing (e.g., Donahue and Moon; Gold; Ritter, *Before*; Masters; Kates). But in this chapter, I posit that work remains to be done to unpack the influence of formal and institutionally specific expectations for student behavior on student writing. En route to finding and interpreting such expectations, we can continue the tradition of recovering and learning from individual professors and students and the tradition of gathering knowledge about general types of institutions (e.g., women's colleges), but emphasis on individuals or on large-scale categories of postsecondary institutions can maintain blind spots about the role of specific institutional configurations in shaping why, how, when, and where students wrote. For example, in *Practicing Writing*, Thomas M. Masters explores broad themes that describe postwar composition practices at three Illinois colleges and universities. He names the colleges and universities that he studied, but focuses on "values and beliefs prized in the academy" (146) rather than another possibility: the values and beliefs nurtured by a student body's institution, whether the small, private, Christian Wheaton College or the large, public land-grant University of Illinois at Urbana-Champaign. By contrast, Kelly Ritter, in *Before Shaughnessy:*

25

Chapter Two

Basic Writing at Yale and Harvard, 1920-1960, creates space for viewing historical writing programs as institutionally specific products, supported by stark differences between Yale and Harvard's early twentieth-century handling of developmental writing. Yale, she finds, separated developmental writing from its regular curriculum, while Harvard acknowledged developmental writing's equal place among its other courses, a difference leading Ritter to propose further study of "local values" affecting a university's categories of students and writing courses (136). Her point echoes Kathleen A. Welsch's study of 1850s college student Mahala Jay, who transferred from Oberlin to Antioch College where Jay followed "the ethnologic of the college," Antioch's honor code (Welsch 19). Yet Ritter leaves many of the local values that she mentions inferred, and Welsch ultimately focuses on Antioch's use of Richard Whately's rhetoric—an intellectual, not an institutional, tradition. Left unfinished is the work of tracing how closely student writing followed behavioral expectations established for students. And composition scholars who have depicted the university itself as a "site for required, enforced behaviors" (Strickland 57; see also Ohmann) have tended to focus broadly, in Donna Strickland's case on the rise of the CCCC's management of composition faculty members across institutions.

The relationship between student writing and institutionally specific expectations for student behavior matters because, first, we now know that part of what students do when they write for academic purposes is try on new roles (Carroll). If students act in new ways through the writing that they produce, we must consider what their actions mean for the students' university. As students write, are they conforming ever-more fully to the behavioral scripts of their university? Are the students normalizing the scripts? Are the students developing a sense of agency apart from their university's expectations? The students' degree of power is vitally important if we wish to discern just how their writing has related and might relate to the institutional setting around them. Second, the relationship between student writing and institutionally specific expectations for student behavior matters because institutional expectations change from institution to institution; therefore, we miss a layer of influence on student writing when we study a broad subject that we call academic values.

Here is where nomos helps. As discussed in Chapter One, nomoi are rules created by people to guide or control human behavior in a specific location, and as neosophistic rhetorical theorists emphasize, rules for language use itself fall into this category. Ken Lindblom states the neosophistic perspective well, I think, when he calls nomoi "continuously renegotiated agreements for the making of meaning that constitutes the work of a particular community" (qtd. in Gillam 55). As social constructs, nomoi can be changed. So as I think about nomoi in terms of student writing at specific universities, my main questions become: what role did students have in "continuously renegotiat[ing] agreements" about how the students should behave? To what extent did student writing show the students upholding, ignoring, or changing existing rules for how the students should act? However, before trying to answer these questions, I want to highlight two additional features of early sophistic understandings of nomoi that I find to have explanatory power today: 1) nomoi could entail beliefs or customs on the one hand or formal codes or laws on the other hand, and 2) nomoi carried power largely because they endorsed someone's or some group's moral values. Classics scholar W.K.C. Guthrie explains that in the fifth-fourth centuries BCE, nomos was "believed in, practiced or held to be right" (56). In "moral or political spheres," many early sophists evoked nomoi by emphasizing "traditional or conventional beliefs as to what is right or true" or by emphasizing "laws formally drawn up and passed, which codify 'right usage' and elevate it into an obligatory norm backed by the authority of the state" (Guthrie 56-57). For instance, in *On Truth*, when Antiphon alludes to people who treat their parents in a particular way or who view self-defense in a particular light (Col. 5 [132-64 H.]), he implies prescriptions about moral behavior under the larger idea of nomos-as-custom or nomos-as-belief. When, in *A Defense on Behalf of Palamedes*, Gorgias calls himself "a great benefactor" for having "written laws, the guardians of justice," among his other contributions to his society (30), he implies prescriptions about moral behavior under the larger idea of nomos-as-law. These examples indicate that by recognizing current customs or beliefs or current rules or laws, one conveys a standard for right thinking or action. So part of the new territory to investigate based on a neosophistic updating of nomos is, what moral implication accompanies one's work to renegotiate current customs or laws?

As site-specific, renegotiated rules carrying moral associations, the ancient concept of nomos can inform a study of nineteenth- and early twentieth-century college student writing. This application brings with it new possibilities, chiefly the possibility that the renegotiation process, and with it a reappraisal of moral associations, will involve students whose tuition dollars keep universities afloat. So as I consider nomoi that affected historical student writing at Ohio University and the University of Houston, I examine nomoi of the kind that Guthrie describes as "laws formally drawn up...which codify 'right usage'": administrative expectations for student behavior enshrined in institutional literature (e.g., in university catalogs). Then I consider nomoi in terms of "conventional beliefs as to what is right or true" (Guthrie)—here the *students'* beliefs about what kind of behavior they should exhibit, as suggested by their writing. By heeding both of these accounts of everyday behavior, I illustrate some of the nuance overlooked in past cultural analyses of composition, and I uncover the kind of agency that students at two institutions demonstrated through their writing.

One of the most noteworthy of my findings is that although OU and UH are contextual opposites, representing vastly different kinds of institutions, regions, and student populations, the interactions between early institutional nomoi and student writing at each site showed marked similarities. The most striking similarity was that through their writing, historical students from OU and UH did not simply follow or overturn the nomoi-as-rules of earlier administrators; rather, students from each university elaborated on earlier nomoi, and their elaborations complicated earlier expectations for student behavior. In other words, students added detail that *extended* or *broadened* what early institutional nomoi encouraged the students to act like. Future studies of student writing in the past or present might take up this analytical thread to see how well this kind of interaction characterizes student writing where the researcher teaches, or to see how other kinds of institutional nomoi, those at historically Christian colleges, for example, influence and are influenced by student writing. If focusing on social class, then researchers should notice that the working-class student population of 1930s-era HJC and UH avoided direct resistance to institutional codes for behavior, despite the defiance shown by many workers elsewhere in the country toward industry managers (e.g., J. Hoover 43). Future studies might also focus on different kinds of artifacts from those that I consider. In the remainder of this chapter, I track the relationship between institutional nomoi and those late-nineteenth- and early twentieth-century student writings that offer the fullest accounts available of student life: a diary and scrapbook in the case of OU and a student newspaper in the case of UH. Like any other historical sources, these can't represent all late-nineteenth-century and early twentieth-century students at OU and all early twentieth-century students at UH, but the sources nonetheless hint provocatively at what many students thought.

THE CASE OF OU

At Ohio University, institutional nomoi governing student life—that is, terms establishing the rules of desirable, and, by implication, morally sound, student behavior—date back to the institution's founding in 1804. However, in light of the fact that nomoi are negotiated and renegotiated as opposed to fixed, a full review of this university's rules across the years is unnecessary. Also, early institutional nomoi gloss over this information. For example, the Ohio Legislature's 1804 "Act Establishing an University in the Town of Athens" says almost nothing about rules for student behavior and gives passing attention merely to the need for a university to promote morality. The only other nod to the university's expectations for student behavior comes when the act adds that Ohio

University's rules will adhere to state and national laws ("Ohio University Charter" 4-5), a point worth heeding given later changes to federal laws pertaining to slavery, women's suffrage, Prohibition, and the like. Then, in the rules adopted in 1814 by the OU Board of Trustees, general warnings appear for students to avoid drunkenness, bars, lies, arguments, lasciviousness, disobedience, and cross-dressing (T. Hoover 27-29), as well as encouragement for students to treat all people respectfully (T. Hoover 28). It was later nineteenth-century catalogs that clarified behavioral expectations from Ohio University, so I turn here for samples of institutional nomoi that influenced students as they wrote and went about their college lives.

The earliest OU catalog that has been retained comes from 1843, and its statements about expected student behavior apply primarily to graduation requirements. But two other points receive close attention: the role of the university's literary societies in shaping students' lives and the degree to which the university, through its geographic location, cultivated moral student behavior. Basically, literary societies were student groups that met regularly, in many cases weekly, to discuss literary works, deliver original orations, debate social and political issues of the day, and socialize; typically, a university had more than one literary society, and they would hold public debates with each other or possibly with the literary societies of other institutions. Accounts from some higher education institutions show literary societies in the late 1800s featuring live music between debates and holding dinners and other social events (Ogren 121), giving us a fuller sense of their contribution to the campus community. In the absence of many other student organizations, literary societies proved popular throughout the 1800s (Ogren 49, 108), and at OU, they were both popular and expected activities for students into the first decades of the 1900s. The 1843 OU catalog's coverage of literary societies spans two sections and notes that the university had two such societies, each with a library holding 1,400 volumes and each society nurturing "habits of extemporaneous speaking" and "the proper modes of conducting business in deliberative assemblies" (*Ohio University Bulletin* 14). A "public contest" (most likely a debate) between the societies marked the end of the winter term, and a public addresses from the societies occurred at the end of the summer term (15). The 1843 catalog's second point of emphasis, morality, appears in the expectation for applicants to the university to have "testimonials of good moral character" (14). While the meaning of this expression goes undefined, the idea of morality returns in a detailed description of OU's location, its setting in the Ohio River Valley called "elevated and healthful" and the university's members called "distinguished for intelligence, refinement, and morality." As an institution that is "removed from the great thoroughfares of travel," the catalog continues, OU "affords the best security to the morals of

Students" (16). This acknowledgment of the university's rural setting encouraged students to focus on ideas and cultivate behaviors that the 1843 catalog associated with morality.

OU's 1872-73 catalog, administered during the writing of a student text that I examine below, again shows the university's two literary societies singled out for recognition. Now the catalog says that the societies give students "exercise in declamation, composition, and debate" and help students "becom[e] familiar with the modes of conducting business in deliberative assemblies" (*Ohio University Bulletin* 22). As in 1843, no other student activities appear in the catalog. And again, the 1872-73 catalog alludes to a vague sense of morality, first when discussing admission to OU: "Testimonials of good character are required from applicants for admission" (22). Subsequent references to morality are new. One of them concerns a rule about absences: "No student is allowed to be absent in term-time without special permission. The absence of a student for even a single recitation, exerts on his progress an evil influence, which is seldom appreciated by parents or guardians" (23). Then, and perhaps surprisingly for this public institution, references to morality appear in terms of required religious involvement: "The students are required to be present at prayers in the College Chapel every morning. Every Sabbath afternoon a lecture on some moral or religious subject is delivered in the Chapel" (23). A difference between references to morality in 1843 and in 1872-73, what we might call a renegotiation in institutional nomoi given the passing of three decades and a national war, is the 1872-73 catalog's substitution of comments about location and morality with comments about money and morality. It cautions parents, "Whatever is beyond a reasonable supply [of money] exposes the student to numerous temptations and endangers his happiness and respectability" (23-24). (Incidentally, we should not overlook the male pronoun *his*.) Gone by this point is the description of Athens, Ohio, as isolated enough to preserve students from vice and distractions.

In sum, the catalogs from 1843 and 1872-73 reveal expectations for OU students to participate in 1) a literary society; 2) recitations in courses; and 3) daily prayers in the chapel, and, very likely, Sunday lectures in the chapel. Finally, students were expected to avoid temptation that the 1843 catalog associated with mobile populations and that the 1872-73 catalog associated with money. With these expectations made plain, I turn to student writing itself to gauge how fully the students followed or changed the nomoi at their institution.

The most detailed pre-1950s writing completed by an OU student while enrolled at the university is an 1873 account of the daily life of one student and her graduating class of six peers (Davis 10). Her writing shows the student and her classmates regularly attending literary society meetings, delivering recitations in classes, and attending church services where they received behavioral advice, sometimes from their professor and university president. Also in keeping with the OU catalogs' prescriptions, the students are depicted as focused on Athens, Ohio, events, not harboring urban longings, and the writer of the 1873 piece alludes to possessing little spending money. However, here is where things get interesting, because even when following the catalogs' expectations, the students depicted in the diary appeared to elaborate on their received behavioral scripts. And in the process of elaborating, of describing and humanizing the actions dictated by university catalogs, the students revised the behaviors expected of them. When we view this and other students' writing about college life in relation to institutional nomoi, I argue, we see students nudging their rhetorical education away from structured formal learning (mere memorizing and reciting) and toward interactions that privileged multiple educational venues and traditions, even spontaneous occasions for learning. Accounts from students' pens show students subtly creating space for new customs to support their rhetorical education.

The first and most detailed piece of OU student writing that I reference is an 1873 diary kept by Margaret Boyd, who in June of that year became her university's first female graduate. Boyd graduated in a class of only seven students total (see Fig. 1), and after her death, her classmate John Merrill Davis affirmed her perspective on OU student life (Davis).

Of course, Boyd cannot speak for the remaining six OU graduates of 1873, but as a member of a disenfranchised group, she must have had an unusually acute perspective on institutional expectations for student behavior. As someone whose very status as a woman deviated from past descriptions of OU students' identities (see the use of *his* in the 1872-1873 *Ohio University Bulletin*), someone who entered the university under the name "M. Boyd" (*Ohio University Bulletin, 1868-1869* 11)—the only student listed without a first name—her success in the institution would have depended on her knowledge of required academic subjects as well as her knowledge of expectations for student behavior. She would have had to be able to answer questions like, where were students expected to go? When? And what were students expected to spend their time doing? We glimpse some of the risks of being female at a previously all-male postsecondary institution in the 1870s Midwest in Olive San Louie Anderson's autobiographically inspired description of a physically harmed female student in *An American Girl, and Her Four Years in a Boys' College* (68). If being female already marked one as an outsider at a newly coed postsecondary institution, then the female student had to show skill in navigating new social and academic spaces. Also, although the writing that OU's Margaret Boyd left behind takes the form of a diary, as opposed to a speech or an essay submitted for a grade, I believe that it should be taken seriously as a composition artifact because Boyd was a college student when she produced it, she discusses her rhetorical education in it, and she viewed the diary as a record of her writing progress. For her first

Figure 1. The Ohio University Class of 1873. Courtesy of the University Archives, Mahn Center for Archives and Special Collections, Ohio University Libraries.

entry, on January 1, 1873, she wrote, "This book was given to me Dec. 25th by sister Kate [i.e., Catherine Boyd]. I must try and write every day. In after years it may be nice to look over. I must try to improve a <u>great deal</u> this year, every way." From January 1 until June of 1873, Boyd wrote about her social and intellectual development at OU, supporting Judy Nolte Temple and Suzanne L. Bunkers' point that nineteenth-century women used diary writing to "shape and control their experiences by means of mastering language" (198). For my purposes, Boyd's diary is most important because it allows me to compare institutional nomoi to student writing about campus life.

Some of the elaborating or nudging of institutional nomoi evident in Boyd's diary appears in her coverage of her interactions with elocution professor William Henry Scott, who taught several classes, including rhetoric, and who had recently become president of the university. Scott attended some of the meetings of an OU literary society, made Boyd recite lessons in class, and on some Sundays preached in church about living well, all indicative of campus activity encouraged by the OU catalogs. Yet as Boyd makes clear, Scott did more than follow these roles blindly, and Boyd and her peers did more than follow orders to listen, read, speak, and write. Like the university president in Anderson's 1878 roman à clef who had "to be all things to all men, and to women, too" (O. Anderson 110), Professor Scott's involvement in Boyd's life extended to a range of activities inside the classroom and out (e.g., visiting her at her home). Through this involvement he became a key figure in her late-college life, helping her reflect on her experiences and see how particular communication challenges pertained to each campus activity that she knew. Overspilling the boundaries of coursework, the rhetorical education that Scott encouraged through modeling, teaching, preaching, conversing privately, and participating in student activities took a whole-person cast fitting Arthur E. Walzer's definition of rhetoric: "Historically, rhetoric is a complete art for shaping students—influencing how they think … how they express themselves … and how they move and sound" (124).

One of the areas of her life that Boyd discusses most often is her weekly participation in a coed literary society, which by then was a common feature of Midwestern and Western institutions (Ogren 110), though progressive Oberlin lagged behind on this point (Fairchild 183). Both what the OU catalog prescribed and more, Boyd's literary society meetings occurred on Friday nights and involved formal agenda items, readings and debates among society members, and social stimulation, occasionally with Professor Scott present. All of these factors appear in Boyd's entry from January 17 when the culmination of her day is the fact that she accompanies a friend to "Society." There she mentions Scott's presence: "Prof. Scott came in just as the president [of the literary society] was giving his decision on the debate." She continues, gesturing to the deliberative

33

and social work of the society, "From the Minutes of preceding meeting [sic] we learn that a vote of thanks was to be given to the Ladies for their donation of table cover [sic]. It seems it was to be in writing and that it was to have been very nice. The committee reports progress, speeches from Scott, Evans and Walker." Indicating the centrality of literary society meetings to her weekly life are references such as these: From February 7: "Stay at home this morning to finish my oration. Go in the afternoon and then to society at night. Carrie [a friend] goes with us, I do not eṉ oy it." March 20: She is examined by Professor Scott in astronomy. That night she attends a meeting of "The Philos" (i.e., the Philomathean Literary Society, one of OU's two main literary societies in 1873) where she reports having "a very nice time. A mock trial in which Ballard [a peer] was tried." The regularity of literary society meetings is still more visible when Boyd alludes to unexpected changes in them, as on April 11: "Ella, Kate and I go to society tonight. I speak 'I know her.' There was a stranger there and I thought I never could get through. Ah! little coward that I be." Elsewhere, Boyd refers to going to literary society meetings with the same two classmates mentioned above. As details of this kind accumulate, they suggest the value that she placed on literary society involvement, for she wrote about that which interested her or contributed to her overall development, as established in her January 1 entry.

But the interpersonal dynamics at literary society meetings quickly allow the meetings to take on a life of their own, apart from OU catalog descriptions—a difference only hinted at when Boyd notes the stranger who attended and frightened her while she was delivering an oration. On Friday, April 25, she depicts a literary society meeting as nearly wild: "We have lots of fun. Some one takes hold of Mc. and pushes him around on the lower hall floor. It is dark and he does not know there is a give along. I call to Ella before he lets go. Well Well Well!!!" Though some of the details elude modern-day readers of Boyd's diary, we can imagine a picture of coed amusement that is physical and playful, and all happening at or just after a literary society meeting. Also, much as Boyd shares social high points at the literary society meetings, she records social low points whose causes we can only guess. On Friday, May 2, for example, she writes, "Ella, Kate and I go to Society. Effa Ballard is there. We stay till it is out but <u>then</u> we do not stay long." The variation in tone and the hints of meaningful interactions render her literary society experience a multifaceted contributor to her whole-person development: structured and probably male dominated, yet also social, lively, and refreshingly diverting.

While nineteenth-century literary societies at all-female education institutions strengthened the social bonds of their participants (Kelley 124), many of these literary societies focused on academic and political work (Kelley; Conway 216). Based on archival research at institutions across the country, Mary Kelley explains that all-female literary societies "acted as schools within schools" because the societies emphasized informal academic work, exposure to more books, and participation in debate (117). As female students contributed to literary societies, she explains, the students "experiment[ed] with subjectivities, which were informed by the advanced education they were pursuing" (Kelley 118). At OU's newly coed literary society, Boyd and other students also experimented with subjectivities; however, based on Boyd's descriptions of individual literary society meetings, that experimentation transcended ordinary academic activity, adding new dimensions to institutional nomoi that encouraged OU students to participate in literary societies. For one thing, Boyd spoke publically while masking her fear, thereby following a male-dominated rhetorical tradition for her generation (Johnson 22), even though her female peers were acknowledged for contributing table decorations for a literary society meeting, thereby following postbellum advice literature that taught women to support and not challenge men (Johnson 71). For another thing, sometimes she interacted joyfully and freely with male and female literary society members alike, as if postponing academic and professional commitments and momentarily escaping expected gender roles.

Furthermore, Boyd's recitations for classes, that is, her demonstrated recall of recently taught information (Connors 45, 77), both followed and elaborated on the catalog's vision of student behavior and that vision's ties to morality at 1873 OU. The recitations' importance to her appears in her diary entry from February 4: "Study and recite, Study and recite [—] what monotony! Sometimes I get tired." In the weeks surrounding this date, she reports reciting in certain buildings, reciting for certain classes (e.g., Mental Science), and reciting for other faculty members when Scott is away on university business. The word *recite* fills many of the diary entries about her academic work. Yet coexisting with and commonly outshining references to her recitations themselves are rich details about the gendered communication environment that she endured and the social networks that sustained her. Near the same time as her "study and recite" entry above, Boyd shares, "Scott wants to know if I ever speak orations. I say, 'no[.]' He says he would like to have me speak an original oration two weeks [from then] if I will. The boys [her classmates] say yes I must" (Jan. 25). Over the next two weeks, she records spending her days writing, to the point of missing a prayer meeting, which was exceedingly rare for her as well as a violation of a strict interpretation of the 1872-73 university catalog. "Vainly I call on the Muses," she laments at one point (Feb. 5). Then, on February 8, she shares the outcome of her preparation: "I speak my oration this morning. O! how I felt. I could not keep from crying all the way home. O dear! A letter from Hugh [probably her brother] tonight just finishes me. I wish I could get mad." As remarkable as this classroom event was for her, whatever the problem's source, is the fact of her classmates seeing her through it. She concludes her February 8 entry by referencing a letter that she received from a classmate, Kate, and Boyd says that later she and a friend named Lucy visited various people and "had a nice time." Later that month, her friend John Merrill Davis "came in [her] room at college." Boyd reports, "I was all alone and we had quite a long talk. He gives me back my oration that he teased from me several weeks ago" (Feb. 24). This note and an entry from the following day provide a sense of closure to her painful oration from early February, for on February 25 a friend gives her a quotation reading "No real progress without pain & labor." Yet perhaps the clearest sign of her rebound from her February 5 oration is when, on February 22, she worries about moving after the end of the school year and adds, as if free-associating, "I fear 'Rip' [a classmate] & I laughed too much in elocution class this morning! He likes candy." This entry is one of many times when her elocution class appeared to serve a purpose larger than the academic.

Other support from her classmates, male and female, persists in the coming months. One such moment, presented in unusual detail, comes on May 24:

> I do not debate as the boys want me to. Scott requests me to write an essay. The boys do not want me to do it but I guess I must. I think myself that Scott might tell me what … he does expect of me, but I will do the best I can any how. I would not have cared so much if the boys had not taken it up so quick[.] They are good & I like them.

Despite the fact that Scott asked her to write an essay, presumably unlike his request to his male students to debate, Boyd's male peers wanted her to join them in debating as they do. Their support led her to care more about this gender-based difference in expectations. Also, verbal support from friends led to a changing of gender restrictions in at least one important instance. On June 17, after having expressed sadness about the masculine word endings on her diploma (which was written in Latin), she wrote that two friends, at least one of whom was male, accompanied her "to Scott's room." She continued, "I tell Scott I do not want a diploma with masculine endings and he says he will have it fixed. We four look it over together and find there are only two words that need changing." Given the gender distinctions that color many of her other interactions, the gender of at least one of Boyd's friends likely mattered for a professor who was accustomed to graduating male students. To this we must note Professor Scott's growing support in the weeks surrounding this event, support expressed in class, church, and individual meetings. A classroom example occurred on Saturday, May 10, the day of her elocution class, when Boyd announces, "I did better on my oration today than I did the last time. Scott rather praised me." By June, she attended a class party at Scott's home where she shares that she had "a nice time" (June 10). On June 18, eight days before her graduation date, she writes, "Had a long walk with Scott today, get back my essay. He says I need not fear about it." Then, four days before her graduation, she mentions a public lecture given at her church by an unnamed speaker who was probably Professor Scott in his role as university president: "[The lecturer] tells the boys that they may well be proud that they belong to the class that contains the first lady graduate. I can hardly keep the tears from my eyes such a day" (June 22).

It is, however, her graduation-day entry that surpasses all her others in conveying the level of support she felt by the end of her school term:

> Day of all days—Commencement day for the class o [sic]. 73 [sic] They all do well. Do not forget any of their pieces. I was so very ~~tired~~ frightened before I went up on the stage that I thought I would fail completely. I did much better than I feared. They cheered me as I went up and I think that helped me. I received two boquets [sic] one from Emma and one from Kate Dana. After we are dismissed so many come to congratulate me. I get tired of it. (June 26)

While of course this scene transcends the protocol for student behavior clarified by earlier catalogs, the same can be said of Boyd's experiences in class, at church, and at her literary society meetings. In her writing, Boyd located her overall college development in venues emphasized by OU catalogs, but many of the experiences that she recorded in the greatest detail were defined by the strength of her social connections: her relationships to her classmates, male and female, and her relationship to her professor and eventual supporter, William Henry Scott. The silliness and joys that she alludes to and the pain that she conveys mark her development into a successful member of her college class, someone who would be lauded very publicly by the time of her graduation. And the range of people from whom she drew comfort and by whom she gauged her progress reminds us of the power of networks to give meaning to one's actions. Using the idea of intergenerational social circulation, feminist theorists have illustrated this point in composition history. For example, Lisa Mastrangelo, in *Writing a Progressive Past: Women Teaching and Writing in the Progressive Era*, teases out connections over time among educators John Dewey and Fred Newton Scott at Michigan and many of their female graduate students who, around 1900, exported the educational theory that they learned from Dewey and Scott to Northeastern women's colleges where they taught (54-55). But a key difference between that example and Boyd's network is that whereas Mastrangelo reveals top-down chains of influence (faculty shaping students), Boyd's account shows influence moving in multiple directions thanks partly to students' efforts to voice their concerns. Sometimes Scott's standards clashed with the desires of students as they tried to accommodate their new female peer, and other women, some of them mentioned in Boyd's diary, soon followed Boyd by graduating from OU. We might read these clashes as nomoi-as-customs exerting pressure on nomoi-as-rules, in which case we may note an undercurrent of different moral options.

If judged beyond the context of her institution, Boyd's difficulties seem still more considerable and her triumphs somewhat modest. She became the first female graduate of Ohio University decades after female students began graduating from nearby Oberlin College. As early as 1859, Oberlin's female students were allowed to read essays that they had written for commencement ceremonies (Fairchild 181). Boyd left her university with less visual grandeur than did the congress gaiters-attired Lydia Short, the second female graduate of Indiana's Butler University, over a decade earlier (Weidner 259). And Boyd's graduation year places her on the eve of the largest demographic change to have affected American higher education in that era: the rise of female students (Soliday, *The Politics* 45-46). So I must stress that I am tracing signs of the interactions that structured the writing and educational outlook of a student in a particular institutional context. At Ohio University, a classical education in the tradition of early nineteenth century educational ideals persisted, and, contrary to the growth seen at newer agricultural and mechanical universities, enrollment stayed low and local through the 1870s. Thus, small accomplishments for a student such as Boyd may be read as breakthroughs, and the fact that Boyd recorded struggles that she managed through her interactions with classmates and faculty suggests many ways to supplement the roles envisioned for students in institutional literature. Evident in the standards to which Boyd and her classmates held themselves was the fact that their educational guidance transcended classroom walls (or any particular group or society's walls), the fact that they received guidance from faculty who had the power to influence university customs (e.g., by revising diplomas), and the fact that many students advocated for the inclusion of a new kind of student, here a female student. These newer standards support modern-day compositionist Sara Webb-Sunderhaus' defense of the "personal connection" students in some writing classes feel when the students talk with their instructor and write about their "thought processes and feelings." Also, the cross-venue emphasis in Boyd's diary is echoed in Webb-Sunderhaus' desire for "multiple support structures that go beyond a writing program" (111).

Showing another push away from strictly regulated learning and toward an unpredictable and interpersonally rich educational environment is a glimpse of student-teacher interactions in the scrapbook of OU student Grosvenor S.

McKee in 1913-14, when many other universities were prioritizing research over teaching and student activities, and when many composition instructors elsewhere were abandoning relationship-building opportunities like individual student conferences in favor of editing student writing (Connors 151). In a page titled "Professors I Have Met," McKee lists "Dr. [Edwin Watts] Chubb," an English professor, as one of his favorite faculty members. McKee mentions general subject areas covered in Dr. Chubb's course ("Eng. Comp." and the English poets Tennyson and Browning) as well as the grade that he earned (B-). But McKee also records aspects of Dr. Chubb that speak to the social environment in which McKee wrote and learned. Dr. Chubb's main hobby, McKee writes, was "Telling jokes and trying to surprise you." To the question of Dr. Chubb's favorite story, McKee writes, curiously, and perhaps with intended incongruity, "Jokes." Following this, McKee lists as the "Most Valuable Lesson" he learned, "Not to turn a joke on him [Dr. Chubb]." These comments could suggest anxiety McKee had in his composition class; perhaps he once suffered embarrassment for having made a joke at Dr. Chubb's expense. But overall, and especially in light of the scrapbook page's commemorative purpose, I read the comments as suggesting an agreeable classroom community. The perspective that McKee shares is corroborated in 1949-1950 by first-year OU student Carol Tyler in *Ohio University in the 1920s: A Social History*, when Tyler, looking three decades backward, writes that students routinely "read their own stories and poems" at Professor Chubb's house. Tyler's and McKee's comments are mere hints, suggestions about the rhetorical experiences created by faculty and students; but alongside Boyd's late-nineteenth-century depiction, they draw attention to students who valued and promoted a whole-person rhetorical education that persisted outside of formally designated learning venues and thrived on social, not just intellectual, exchanges.

THE CASE OF UH

To discuss institutional nomoi of the University of Houston before the 1950s, one must remember that UH was founded as Houston Junior College (HJC) in 1927 by the Houston Independent School District (HISD), an arrangement reflecting national trends in the administration of public junior colleges in the late 1920s (Witt et al. 48). From 1927 to 1945, the HISD continued to govern HJC, which became UH in 1934. However, HJC/UH lacked a campus of its own until the late 1930s, initially holding classes at night in Houston's San Jacinto High School and later in a local Baptist church. So institutional nomoi that I examine for this higher education institution come from HISD Superintendent Edison Ellsworth Oberholtzer. (Few details remain in catalogs from

Chapter Two

the 1920s, and yearbooks from the 1930s, the earliest period available, reiterate Superintendent Oberholtzer's vision.) To the superintendent's expectations I compare the first set of detailed student writing available from HJC: 1920-1930s pieces written for the student newspaper *The Cougar*. Like Boyd's diary and McKee's scrapbook in the case of OU, many of the *Cougar* articles describe HJC and UH student life itself.

In research collected in the late 1940s, UH Associate Professor James Chester Cochran, supported by records from former Superintendent and later UH President Oberholtzer (Cochran iii), described UH's philosophy as "emphasiz[ing] those educational services growing out of the individual and community educational needs of the citizens of the area" (Cochran 1), a philosophy consonant with many of the junior colleges founded in the 1920s (Witt et al. 40). Categorizing UH as a municipal university, which "operate[s] under some phase of municipal control and serv[es] the local educational needs of a city and its contributing territories (2-3), Cochran linked UH's *raison d'etre* to the practical and cultural needs of Houston by offering classes of interest to the city's prominent industries. In addition to serving nearby industry needs, he continued, municipal universities and junior colleges link city school districts to higher education: "The establishment of [municipal universities or junior colleges] means, in effect, the extension upward of the local public school system. Each has been established for the purpose of extending the privileges of higher education to those for whom they would not otherwise be available" (Eckelberry qtd. in Cochran 14). The link to local public schools was seconded in a 1948 article in the *Texas Outlook*, a publication of the Texas State Teachers Association, which called the Houston Junior College of 1927 to 1934 a "branch of the Houston public schools" (Patterson 11).

Official UH records that I see as nomoi-as-rules show the institution fitting this description. The charter from the HISD Board of Trustees, published in 1934, framed UH as necessary "to provide a background for intelligent citizenship" (qtd. in Oberholtzer 23). It added that to help "our citizens meet the issues of life," the citizens must "develop the qualities of open-mindedness, adaptability, and a willingness to work together for the common welfare. Although individual initiative must be maintained, citizens of a truly democratic society must become aware of the evils of selfishness and narrow individualism" (qtd. in Oberholtzer 23). In 1945, after the Board of Regents assumed "active duty" of UH (Oberholtzer 29), the university's mission was "to serve all the educational needs of the citizens of this community" (31). It is important to realize that these references to citizens and the community meant, first and foremost, Houston citizens and the Houston community. On January 17, 1944, for example, the UH Board of Trustees voted to make "courses adapted, in length and content, to the demands for trained personnel for Houston business and industry" (qtd. in Oberholtzer 60), and Houston's continuing growth kept demand high for trained personnel.

The interests permeating the statements about UH above correspond to the earlier vision of HJC attributed to President Oberholtzer and HJC dean F.M. Black and summarized in a March 7, 1927 *Houston Chronicle* article. There, HJC's aims were presented as follows:

> To accommodate the large number of high school graduates with limited means.
>
> To enable boys and girls who must work at jobs during the day to attend college after working hours in the evening.
>
> One of the great aims of the Junior College is to offer vocational, trade, and business training to those who have no intention of going to college.
>
> To offer an opportunity to the more mature adult group who wish to attend class purely for the love of learning.
>
> The Junior College will be able to adapt its courses to local needs.
>
> To provide pre-professional training for students who plan to enter professional schools. (Watts qtd. in Cochran 33)

Oberholtzer and Black grounded this educational experience in terms of accessibility, practicality, and student and worker proximity, terms indicating the kind of student that they anticipated and the kind of education that this student would receive. He or she would already have a job, would make time for college at night, would pay little for college, and would value skills that had caché in Houston. Thus planned, HJC grew into the most populous junior college in Texas by 1928 (Cochran 51-52).

By 1934 when HJC became UH, the institution's student body appeared similar to the student population anticipated in 1927. The majority of UH's students came from local public schools (University of Houston Administration), showing that demographic data from this time matched university leaders' vision. Also, from 1934 to 1944, the most bachelor's degrees awarded at UH went to students who majored in education, with English second and business administration third (ibid). The output of educators and business leaders fit the university's mission; so did the high number of English majors once we see that at this time "English majors" included students who wrote newspaper articles and edited the university yearbook.

Chapter Two

This leaves student writing: did it mimic and thus maintain institutional nomoi by portraying HJC as an extension of local public schools and as attentive to the practical and cultural needs of Houston? To an extent, yes. However, HJC students did more than follow an existing script; in their writing, the students also pushed to make HJC appear distinct from nearby primary and secondary schools and from local businesses and industries. In stressing HJC's differences, students supported feelings of institutional pride and, as at OU, located their education amid memorable teacher-to-student and student-to-student interactions. The students' views during HJC's early years are important because they show students complicating the terms of their rhetorical education, and nowhere was their work to complicate more apparent than in their writing for the student newspaper *The Cougar*, writing that counted for academic credit and dwelt on students' experiences.

To be sure, *one* way that students discussed their writing and other educational experiences at HJC was by centralizing the new institution's connectedness to the HISD and to local business and industry. The recurrence of these references testifies to the power of institutional expectations to shape how students see themselves. In the 1929-published "Education," a typical article publicizing HJC's local connections, student Helen Cheney lauds HJC for its distinctive service to the local school district. She writes that the HJC is the "only institution in Houston offering the education courses that are required before a person may enter the city system," and she adds that many Rice University students attend HJC for this reason. Her institutional hype hinges on HJC's attraction to other Houston organizations: Rice University and the public school system. Also common in *The Cougar*'s early issues are pieces that introduce HJC administrators while also foregrounding HJC-HISD connections. For example, a 1928 article on Dean F.M. Black shares the fact that Black had supervised Houston's secondary schools and overseen the building of San Jacinto High School where he served as principal and where HJC held its first classes ("F.M. Black"). Given the associations conveyed in the article about Dean Black, one's qualifications to uphold expectations at HJC appear to stem from one's nearness to the HISD.

Yet this is not the only or even the most prominent narrative in *The Cougar*. Troubling the institutional nomoi that foregrounded links to local industry and the local school system is the fact that within a few years of HJC's founding, students highlighted characteristics of their education that lacked direct links to surrounding organizations. In some cases, the students asserted the uniqueness and worth of their college education by touting HJC apart from its surroundings. Today's readers might criticize the sensationalism common in newspaper articles from the early twentieth century, but this genre also facilitated students' revisions of institutional nomoi. In at least two ways, students who wrote for

The Cougar broadened the idea that, as HJC students, they should further the common (Houston-area) good, train in ways needed by nearby businesses and industries, and treat their education as an extension of a Houston public schools education. First, the students portrayed their rhetorical achievements as commendable in their own right, regardless of needs from the surrounding city. Second, the students highlighted faculty members who created a unique rhetorical education apart from demands of local businesses, industries, and K-12 educators. In short, the students used their newspaper to assert a version of HJC whose significance transcended mere proximity to Houston-based organizations.

In tone, subject matter, and organization, 1920s-1930s articles in *The Cougar* treated HJC students' lives and achievements as intrinsically worthy topics. Pictorial indications of a new identity emerged in 1928 when the paper began featuring a cartoonish image of a cougar across the top of the front page, and when, in the same issue, the paper featured numerous articles urging HJC students to show more school spirit, a stronger collective identity. By April 1929, one issue of *The Cougar* featured front-page articles with titles that spoke loudly and collectively (see Fig. 2): "Status of Junior College Important," "State Recognizes Work Completed at Junior College," "Municipal College Shows Progress in Educational Field" (with the subtitle "History of Houston Junior College Replete With Scholastic Achievement"), "Scholastic Rating of Junior College Above the Average" (*The Cougar*, 1929).

Granted that articles about status and ranking refer to relationships to other institutions, these articles nevertheless downplay the narrative of HJC serving HISD and local business interests and instead support a newer narrative of HJC creating valuable educational experiences. A distinct institutional identity is also suggested by the newspaper editors' decision to place the April 1929 issue's front-page articles around a large, centered article about President and HISD Superintendent Oberholtzer—accompanied by his picture (ibid). If this arrangement failed to convey a new sense of HJC's educational value, readers could flip to student testimonials such as Bruce Manley's "Junior College Best Preparation for Life of Higher Education":

> When I finished high school I was thoroughly tired of staying at home. Accordingly, a few months later I was standing in line in front of the registrar's office at a university over 2000 miles from home.
>
> I entered the University of Michigan positively knowing that I wanted to become a geologist. When I returned home this past summer, I had lost all interest in ever becoming a geologist, did not care whether or not I ever finished college.

Chapter Two

Figure 2. *The Cougar*, April 1929. Courtesy of the Archives and Special Collections, University of Houston.

> The first few months I was at the university I was completely
> lost. My best efforts were usually rewarded with low grades.
> At final examination all the freshmen were worried. Accidents
> do happen, however, for some of us were allowed to stay.
>
> From my own experiences, I believe that by going to a junior
> college first, a student should have no such difficulties when
> he later enters a distant college. In the first place, the professors in a junior college take much more interest in the
> students because the classes are small. The professors give only
> short lectures at first, thus accustoming the students to taking
> notes on long lectures. By waiting a couple of years before
> entering a larger college, a student is more mature and better
> able to judge what he wants his life work to be. I feel that
> by going to junior college this year I have learned a number
> of things that will improve the character of my work when I
> return to the University of Michigan next fall.

Manley, whose educational commitment is cemented by his tie to the older and better-known University of Michigan across the country, adds to the other articles' message by mentioning small class sizes, professors' interest in students, and the need for students to consider learning and life options. His experience also supports institutional nomoi concerning HJC's role in providing practical higher education options for local students, but this constitutes one of many points supported by his narrative.

More jubilant and prescriptive articles followed that encouraged students to serve as advertisers of HJC. "Be Booster," an anonymous article from December 1929—months after the stock market crash that ushered in the Great Depression—explained,

> Many high school students judge the College by the actions
> and words of their friends who are now enrolled there. *Let
> your words and your actions show that you are attending a real,
> live college, and that you are proud of your school.* If you can not
> get this attitude, why are you here? Better far that you should
> get out and try some other institution, where you may find
> matters even less to your liking. (emphasis added)

If before this period students selected topics and organized articles to imply a new direction for the identity of HJC students, now students called directly for their fellow students to show pride or leave. The idea of attending HJC purely for the sake of convenience (e.g., family ties, low living and tuition costs) appears unacceptable to the writer or writers of "Be Booster." Now students were requested to identify unabashedly with a college that had not even existed a few years earlier.

Given the plethora of articles emphasizing HJC students' accolades and positive opinions, what else might readers need in order to see HJC as a distinct and valuable entity for reasons beyond its local economic and educational contributions? By the early 1930s, one answer became student organizations, the rise of which reflected national trends among junior colleges (Witt et al. 105). At HJC, many of the student organizations blended intellectual work with social engagement in ways comparable to the literary societies experienced by OU's class of 1873. In 1933, oratory and theater assumed the most prominent places on the front page of HJC's *The Cougar*, to the point that by November the newspaper led with an article on the Dramatic Club. By February 1934, front-page articles covered numerous student activities, and by March 1934, the largest and most prominently featured front-page article addressed an upcoming debate that would be followed by a school dance. This article ends with the statement, "The contest has been arranged for the night of the Freshman Dance so that those attending the debate may go the [sic] dance which will begin at ten o'clock at the University Club building" ("Junior College" 4). As these examples indicate, students presented academic contests and social bonding together, and without attempting to link them to Houston's educational and economic needs. Also emphasizing HJC-facilitated social life, students added front-page articles on a sophomore prom, a speakers' club, and pro and con perspectives on dancing. On the front page of one November 1933 issue alone, readers find updates on the Science Club, the Outdoor Club, the Dramatic Club, and the Honor Society, as well as announcements of academic and athletic achievements (*The Cougar*, 1933).

The fact that contributors to *The Cougar* dwelt on organizations and events that encouraged the building of intra-institutional, not just inter-institutional, relationships indicates a movement—organized or intuited, direct or indirect—to modify earlier depictions of HJC students as trainees of local businesses and education interests. By implication, the movement created a different moral standpoint, suggesting that a focus on institutional identity building is good or right. Writing from *The Cougar* turns more decidedly in this direction given its additional focus on the popularity and amiability of individual HJC professors. This is the case when a Harvey W. Harris, instructor of "English and public speaking" and "chairman of the [HJC] Social Committee," is quoted about HJC's appeal in an article titled "English Prof Has Praise for College" (Shepperd). Harris, who "will be in charge of the English department during the summer term," is quoted as saying, "I understand there is quite a demand being made for the second half of sophomore English … and I feel that in case sufficient demand is made for it the administration will offer the course" (qtd. in Shepperd). By 1934, professors were singled out as spokespeople for all the courses that they taught, acting nearly as salespeople. In a section of the newspaper called "Rambling Reporter," appearing soon after HJC's transformation to the University of Houston (UH), one finds:

> Visit Mr. Holt's classes and you will wish you could squeeze in a period with him. He even makes poetry interesting. In expounding the whys and wherefores of poetry he finds place for little interesting or humorous happenings that lend a ready explanation to some point. He says "Poetry is like olives, you [sic] have to cultivate a taste for it."

Accompanying this enticement is an invitation to visit faculty member L. Standlee Mitchell's English class to be entertained by his jokes. (Although it can't support broad conclusions, the fact that some early-twentieth-century students at both OU and HJC/UH praised English professors for their jokes indicates one way in which student-instructor relationships developed.) Another enticement in "Rambling Reporter" appears in a humorous description of Professor Harris's popularity: "Due to an overcrowded condition in Public Speaking I, the class has been divided into three sections with a chairman over each section. Mr. Harris, instructor, tries to be present in all three of these classes simultaneously, and comes nearer to accomplishing that feat than one might think."

The tradition above continued and intensified in subsequent issues. For example, in late 1934, Mr. Holt is singled out as follows:

> Professor Holt, instructor of English, is one of the most charming and pleasing personalities at the University. He presents his course in an interesting manner, commenting frequently on the poem or author under discussion. Not only does Mr. Holt explain the poem to the n'th [sic] degree, but he also adds that personal touch concerning his views on the philosophy of the poem.
>
> Mr. Holt has an excellent sense of humor and finds something humorous in the most serious poetry. All students enrolled in his classes are beginning to think seriously of the meaning of 'fatalism' and its outcome. ("Personal")

In examples such as this, students emphasize the worth of particular courses by describing their professors' charisma, frequently their humor. What emerges as the trend continues is a picture of HJC/UH as an organization whose students and faculty control the education to be found therein, an organization that, while connected to a larger city, should be experienced for the mini-societies that it cultivates.

Featuring more articles in the late 1920s and early 1930s than I can analyze here, *The Cougar* fails to support a single conclusion about how students portrayed HJC and the literacy practices encouraged therein. Even as some articles spotlighted new interactional possibilities at the college, other articles continued to discuss HJC's value in terms of its ability to meet "a need in the community" and its "distinct usefulness in the educational system of the city," as one 1932 article put it ("Dear Old College"). What is important for my purposes is the fact that both of these trends coexisted, creating a discursive environment where students' visions of themselves and their education began to fill prime sections of the newspaper. Much as the cases of OU's Margaret Boyd and Grosvenor S. McKee show students nudging institutional nomoi in a new direction, contributions to HJC's *The Cougar* show students acknowledging and broadening President Oberholtzer's vision of students' educational purposes and priorities. These are not cases of students revolutionizing their rhetorical education, but cases of students using writing to re-center, slightly but significantly, the terms of their rhetorical education. Evidence from OU and UH shows students moving away from officially recognized identities and actions and toward personally meaningful approaches to their rhetorical education.

CROSS-SITE LESSONS

As discussed in Chapter One, composition scholars and instructors seeking to make sense of where they teach may feel paralyzed when faced with seemingly limitless possibilities for studying the notion of place, whether place is conceptualizing as a rhetorical ecology (Rice) or as "activities, actors, situations, and phenomena [that] are conceived as independent, diverse, and fused through feedback" (Fleckenstein et al. 389). Where does one start? Which "activities, actors, situations" and so on should one select? Based on the evidence in this chapter, one viable starting place could be tracking the nomoi underlying students' actions in college (institutional nomoi) as well as the nomoi that students endorse, perhaps informally or indirectly, as they work together to elaborate on institutional nomoi. With this done, one may look for tensions between the assumed goodness or rightness of each nomos. Even if, through their writing and other rhetorical activities, college students adjust institutional nomoi only slightly, that adjustment creates an opportunity to examine new convictions that aren't immediately or necessarily preserved in institutional literature about the direction in which a university should head and about the kind of students or student-writers a university should produce. If nomos-as-custom never manages to become nomos-as-rule, then that yields another dynamic to explore. This analytical thread accentuates *one* set of interactions—students' interactions with institutional codes—that scholars and instructors may take up and consider at other institutional sites without denying the many factors in play when a writer writes. The thread positions scholars and instructors to speak back to local histories of composition by asking how academic values (Masters 146) and "local values" (Ritter, *Before Shaughnessy* 136) have played out institutionally; how institutional discourses such as guidelines for student behavior have been interpreted by particular students or by particular classes or generations of students; and how personal writing (e.g., diaries, scrapbooks), journalism (e.g., articles, advertisements), or other writing genres have enabled students to suggest new ways of acting and identifying.

While I will return to pedagogical applications in Chapter Six, a productive starting point for writing teachers who attend to present-day interactions of student writing and institutional expectations is to ask, what expectations for student behavior are upheld by my institution, and how do those expectations differ from expectations found at other institutions? With this known, one can ask, how are my students, through their writing, interacting with their institutional expectations? If alignment between the two isn't visible, an instructor could study strategies by which students construct different visions of themselves and reasons for attempting such revisions. An implication for teaching is that instructors may want to think more deliberately about the relationship between their (institutionally informed) teaching goals and the writing environments that they cultivate in classes and in other areas of student life. Ultimately, the instructor who investigates these issues would be thinking about context, but to stop here, with the notion of context, allows the instructor to overlook the specific interactional qualities that this chapter's analysis of student writing at OU and UH has surfaced.

Of course, any analysis suffers from "incompleteness and distortions" (Fleckenstein et al. 389), in this case by elevating one set of relationships over other sets of relationships. So I accept the sophistic tenet of *dissoi logoi*, or opposing arguments, by turning now to a historical analysis that privileges a broader set of interactions: student writing and once-current issues for the students' surrounding state or city.

CHAPTER THREE

TRACKING LINES OF COMMUNICATION: STUDENT WRITING AS A RESPONSE TO CIVIC ISSUES

Writing of all kinds is connected to so many people, ideas, and things that untangling and studying its locatedness might seem manageable only through thick description or broad theorizing. In this chapter as elsewhere, I strive to occupy a space between these two positions, using concepts with sophistic roots to elevate one connection at a time between college student writing and its surroundings. As Chapter Two showed, one connection worth tracking between college student writing and other people and ideas is the writing's connection to nomoi that have dictated desirable student behaviors in the area where the writing was initiated and completed. Studying this set of relationships can highlight behaviors that are requested by institutional power holders as well as behaviors from students on the ground, so to speak, students who, through their writing, amended received behavioral scripts. But studying other connections between college student writing and its surroundings can support more understandings of the writing's spatial work.

In this chapter, I examine some of the ideological work of student writing in the late 1800s to early 1900s in the case of OU and from the late 1920s to the mid 1940s in the case of UH, periods when each university fought to clarify its purpose to itself and others in the wake of surrounding growth. To accomplish this, I unpack the relationship between student writing and an emerging cultural region in the case of OU and the relationship between student writing and an emerging metropolitan area in the case of UH. At OU, college student writing in many genres and venues can be framed as a collective response to the social isolation and political marginalization that engulfed southeastern Ohio, and indeed much of the area now called Appalachia, from the late 1800s to the early 1900s. In Houston, early-twentieth-century college student writing of various genres can be framed as a collective response from working and nontraditional college students to a city population that had not systematically heeded this group's perspectives in civic discussions. Thus, I frame student writers as attentive to coursework at the same time that the students attended to geographically specific political, economic, and cultural conditions. Although students at OU and UH submitted most of their writing for academic credit, I argue that the students were also submitting ideas to a surrounding populace, ideas through which the students sought to represent other students at their institution.

This chapter's focus on responsiveness is informed by kairos, frequently taken to mean the timeliness of a message, and a concept preceding even the First Sophists. The author of *Dissoi Logoi* quotes an ancient verse containing the clause "there is nothing that is in every respect seemly or shameful, but the *Right Moment* takes the same things and makes them shameful and then changes them round and makes them seemly" (50, emphasis added). Later, the writer draws on the line from Aeschylus "there are occasions when God respects an opportune moment for lies" (51). These examples point to opportunities for actions that may be judged any which way depending on the interplay of custom and timing. Gorgias shows his devotion to kairos in his *Encomium of Helen* and *Defense on Behalf of Palamedes*, and, as scholars have argued, implies many ways in which kairos works (D. Sullivan 318-19; Sipiora 18-19). He observes, "It has happened that people, after having seen frightening sights, have also lost presence of mind for the present moment" (Gorgias, "*The Encomium*" 17), and, at a formal defense before a court, he says that "the present occasion requires" him to create a defense filled with self-praise (Gorgias, "*A Defense*" 32). Here he ties one type of witnessed event to a temporary moment of disturbed feeling and a high-stakes social situation to the necessity for a particular line of reasoning. By extension, it would seem that each other sight or social gathering supports a unique moment of feeling or response. If Gorgias also wrote a treatise titled *Peri Kairou*, or *On the Right Moment in Time*, a possibility acknowledged by several scholars (e.g., Sipiora 4; Kerferd 45), then we have little room to doubt that a time-bound version of kairos lay at the heart of his teachings.

Gorgias' views on kairos hold even for much recent scholarship. In the 1980s and 1990s when John Poulakos analyzed key concepts undergirding ancient sophistic teachings, he found that one of the main ideas underlying the First Sophistic enterprise was *kairoi*, or "opportune rhetorical moments" created or used by people to act in a unique situation (*Sophistical* 61). Studying speech as opposed to writing, Poulakos stressed the temporally disruptive dimension of kairos: "The rhetor who operates mainly with the awareness of kairos responds spontaneously to the fleeting situation at hand, speaks on the spur of the moment, and addresses each occasion in its particularity, its singularity, its uniqueness" (ibid). His focus on situation, with its similarity to Lloyd Bitzer and Richard Vatz's debate circa 1970 about the rhetorical situation, is shared by others, including Bruce McComiskey, who, in *Gorgias and the New Sophistic Rhetoric*, called kairos the act of "seizing the opportune moment, choosing arguments depending on the demands of the situation" (111). If accepted without further qualifiers, these definitions keep kairos tied to speech.

Of course, the fact that I am studying writing places different demands on conventional appropriations of kairos. Writing sticks around beyond one exchange and, as Jenny Edbauer Rice has shown, may be reused or repurposed beyond a single moment in the service of various goals. So to adapt conventional understandings of kairos to a student writing milieu, I extend a point that McComiskey makes about the role of language in questioning and disrupting discursive systems. In the final chapter of *Gorgias and the New Sophistic Rhetoric*, as he analyzes the rhetoric of the global community, McComiskey deemphasizes communication situations that are bounded by clear timeframes and emphasizes rhetoric that speaks back to particular regulatory circumstances. Building on Michel de Certeau's concept of tactics, McComiskey writes,

> [kairos] speaks not of argument from institutional authority, not of an immutable base from which relations to others might be consistently managed; it speaks not a discourse of globalization, as Plato and others did, but a discourse of uncertainty, a discourse of tactics among powerful strategic discourses. Kairotic arguments do not dictate; they respond. (113, emphasis added)

When power is taken into account, according to this explanation, a *kairotic* argument becomes a specific wielding of language to problematize existing relations. For example, one might use writing to expose connections and interests that were previously hidden by socially privileged discourses.

McComiskey does not forget timeliness and situation. Still he defends "tactics that harness the power of the right moment, that restrict their interventions to the specificity of particular situational contexts" (115-16) so as to diminish the tactics' cooptation by regulatory systems. But once he finishes unpacking kairotic action from the angles of hegemony and globalization, the "right moment" suggests a myriad of options. In one of his concluding points, a comparison of critical tactics and productive tactics, he gives the following summary of culture and change: "Cultures evolve through the production of texts, and if enough subversive texts are entered into the flow of cultural production, then the culture itself will change *gradually*, incorporating subversive ideas into the very fabric of its own process" (117, emphasis added). When he then endorses "tactics that, a little at a time, work toward challenging marginalizing strategies" and quotes Theodor Adorno's line "steady drops hollow the stone" (117), he allows for the possibility that today we can consider several right moments, or several right days or years, for subversive texts to effect cultural change. To this, I would stress that if focusing on writing, as in pre-1950s college student writing, we find more reasons to relax speech-oriented notions of *timeliness* and *situation* and instead notice the steady local work of texts to create a narrative seeking cultural change. Below, I examine historical student writing in terms of its responsiveness to existing social conditions, and I argue that one may act kairotically, in the tactical sense noted above, despite whether one responds directly and immediately, within a single fleeting moment. My evidence suggests that students at OU and UH responded in multiple waves to an originating issue: in the case of OU, the decision of nineteenth-century Ohio state legislators to direct educational funds to institutions other than Ohio University, and in the case of UH, the decision of the Houston Independent School District to create and govern two junior colleges for this city's population. In this way, a conception of kairos updated to reflect college student writing can support another angle by which scholars and instructors interpret composition's spatial work, an angle revealing composition's ideological contributions to rural or metropolitan region making.

COUNTERING REGIONAL NEGLECT AT OU

OU student writing in the decades surrounding 1900 shows students, increasingly students who came to OU from industrializing areas in the north and west, writing about sites and issues of special importance to OU, Athens, and rural, hilly southeastern Ohio. While today we lack access to academic essays written by students across the years and to most of the teaching materials of the students' writing instructors, clues from literary societies, student newspapers, creative pieces, student theses, and, by the 1940s, certain pedagogical materials reveal a unifying theme in the writing experiences of OU students from the mid 1800s to the early 1900s: generations of OU students investigated connections among themselves, their institution, and the surrounding town and region. Taking no one form or approach, their investigations encouraged readers to reflect on the significance of OU, Athens, and southeastern Ohio as the students interacted with these areas. Although late-twentieth-century Rhetoric and Composition scholars have shown that numerous American colleges and universities circa 1900 prompted students to write about familiar, observable topics (Connors 64; Kitzhaber 108), an analysis that considers state-level changes from the late 1800s shows that early OU students did more than fulfill class or extracurricular expectations when they wrote about the value of their university and its environs. The students also acted kairotically—tactically, from university-specific perspectives and in response to specific political conditions. The recurrence of this tendency across time and forms gives those of us teaching and studying writing today a fuller understanding of what it means for college students' academic or classroom writing to do extra-academic work.

One of the issues dominating the history of higher education in dramatically growing nineteenth-century Ohio is the fact that state leaders had to make difficult decisions about how to fund an overabundance of postsecondary institutions, and civic and education leaders from all parts of the state worked to obtain whatever funding and political and economic goodwill they could get. In light of these state-level dealings, locally focused OU student writing in the decades around 1900 can be seen as a strategic series of responses to state leaders who had begun allocating significant amounts of education funding and related support to new postsecondary institutions in central, northern, and western Ohio. I argue that it became more than a fulfillment of course or extracurricular duties when OU students created positive portrayals of Athens and the surrounding land and when students used their writing to expose the area's challenges. The students were not writing political pamphlets and organizing within a single academic term or year, but nevertheless the students responded to feelings of sociopolitical neglect that were descending upon OU, Athens, and southeastern Ohio in the wake of Ohio's nineteenth-century growth.

By the mid-late 1800s, the oratorical and classical tradition of education still found at OU as at many other colleges and universities paralleled state developments such as the rise of Columbus, Cleveland, Cincinnati, Akron, Dayton, and Toledo, all north or west of Ohio University, as hubs of state commerce, industry, and politics. Throughout the same period, political leaders from the earlier-settled southeastern corner of the state saw their requests for tax revenue and other resources dismissed by the state legislature (Peters; T. Hoover). In 1869, one OU alumnus who became active in Athens civic groups wrote, "At the present time [OU] is with difficulty sustained and its condition is no credit to the State" (Walker qtd. in Super 29). The alumnus attributed the conditions of the university to the state legislature's "mismanagement and trickery," which, as early as the 1840s, kept OU from revenue from the university's land reappraisals (ibid; see also T. Hoover 78). Charles William Super, president of OU from 1884 to 1896 and 1899 to 1901, added his disappointment that nineteenth-century families in the entire Athens area experienced poor educational conditions. He wrote,

> There is considerable evidence to the effect that the children in the new environment [in and around Athens, Ohio] grew up less intelligent and less interested in knowledge than their parents. Most of the latter had acquired something more than the rudiments of an education in the "East," although the term East must be somewhat liberally interpreted. They carried with them into the wilderness some of the books they

> owned. We also see from the autobiography of Thomas Ewing [one of OU's first alumni] that they took infinite pains to increase their scanty store. When these books were lost or worn out they were often not replaced. (30)

Weaving between Athens-area families and OU specifically, Super wrapped OU and its environs in a narrative of decline. A later historian wrote that although some of the earliest settlers in Ohio thought OU would "become one of the great American universities," the institution instead suffered through "years of hardship and frustration, limited facilities, enrollments, and equipment" (T. Hoover 79). Based on these accounts from politically and historically aware local residents, we might ask, were OU students likely to have similar concerns?

Although late-nineteenth-century and early-twentieth-century OU student writing that remains today includes poetry, descriptions, and newspaper articles, not manifestos or letters to state leaders, the fact that the students wrote favorable pieces about local sites and issues while intrastate disputes about educational resources and status persisted reveals possible influences on their writing. One example of the intrastate disputes was an extended written debate in and around the 1870s between a heritage society called the Athens County Pioneer Association and a well-known Cincinnati publisher. This exchange, involving numerous letters sent between these two parties and to other historical authorities, hinged on whether the location of the state's first library was in Athens County in southeast Ohio or in Cincinnati in (the more urbanized and industrialized) southwest Ohio. The exchange, which suggests the importance of regional location on state discourses, led to a discussion about historical sources and about definitions of terms like *first* and *library* (Athens County). A second, university-based example of intrastate tensions concerned the relationship between advocates for OU's financial interests and advocates for The Ohio State University's (OSU's) financial interests. OU President Super went as far as to portray OU's late-1800s trustees as "either inside the fort defending [OU] against enemy onslaughts or on the outside trying to collect the [monetary] tribute which they claimed was justly their due" (26). With OU presented as a "fort" guarding against "enemy onslaughts," Super bemoaned OU's financial conditions as the state grew and saw its higher education needs multiply. For scholars today, placing intrastate disputes such as these alongside locally focused OU student writing from the same time period reveals how neatly student writing that praised or defended OU, Athens, or southeast Ohio fit into a larger tradition of Athens and southeastern Ohio residents seeking support, or at least recognition, from a state population that increasingly valued newer social and commercial centers. As I explain below, student writing across the same time period added "steady drops" in an effort to "hollow the stone," to return to Adorno's metaphor of social change as gradual and collective.

Some of the earliest OU student writing that has survived either blended writing with oratory (as was common in the mid 1800s) or did journalistic work; in both cases students documented or even defended their college environs, encouraging reflection about the relevance of their university, Athens, or southeastern Ohio. While literary societies at other institutions focused on debates about national social issues and about the value of historical figures and intellectual contributions (Ogren 49-50), students in OU's Philomathean Literary Society in 1837-38 made room to debate questions such as, "Is Athens a suitable situation for a literary institution?" (qtd. in J. White 38), and students in the Athenian Literary Society in 1843 debated the question, "Should the O.U. [sic] be removed from Athens?" in addition to expected topics (qtd. in J. White 57). The latter year also saw the student-run newsletter *The Echo and University Record* publish an essay titled "Removal of the College," in which students reported on a proposal from state legislators to move OU to central or northern Ohio. The writers of "Removal of the College" supported a move to the geographic center of Ohio, concluding, "Then, and *not till* then will the Ohio University take a rank among the Literary Institutions of the land, consistent with its lofty name and the character of the distinguished men who conduct its affairs" ("Removal").

The next mass-distributed writing from OU students that has been retained comes from the 1870s when, in volume one of *The Student's Magazine*, unidentified students push for town-and-gown relations that interweave the interests of OU students and other Athens residents. The students write, "A word to the people of Athens. The interests of the Town and College are inseparable; and if the College is benefited by the publication of a journal, so also is the Town. And so much as the citizens encourage and aid us, just so much do they advance their own interests" ("Editorials" 25). Shortly thereafter, the writers make a case for how *The Student's Magazine* can portray OU and its various supporters: "We now promise on our part that if we receive fair patronage and aid…[we will] use our utmost endeavors to see that the MAGAZINE reflects no discredit on the institution which it represents, and to make it worthy the support of its friends" (25). In turn, these writers continue, OU students can make a point of supporting nearby businesses:

> The business men [sic] who encourage us by advertising should in return receive the patronage of the students … [Local businesspeople] desire and expect some income from their patronage, and we should do our part that they be not disappointed.

> Let every student then, who has any interest in the welfare of the MAGAZINE, and of the college, notice our advertising columns, and bestow his patronage accordingly. (26)

The article's depiction of Athens residents frames students and non-students as capable of supporting each other, reminding readers that patronage can work in multiple ways. Also, the refusal of the article writers to isolate OU students' interests from the interests of nearby townspeople carries over to later depictions of the Athens area.

Among *The Student's Magazine* more glowing pieces about OU-Athens-southeast Ohio was its 1880 reprint of the poem "Athens, Ohio," written by 1833 alumnus and Marietta, Ohio, native William Dana Emerson probably during or soon after his student years. The poem's reappearance in *The Student's Magazine*, then in President Super's 1924 history of OU and in 1920s university bulletins shows one way that generations of OU affiliates, students, and university leaders attempted to maintain or advance an image of OU-Athens-southeast Ohio as a center of education and idyllic natural scenes. Nearly every line in the poem praises Athens and its surroundings, and I find it likely that what Gorgias had called "the present occasion" requiring praise ("*A Defense*" 32) spanned a series of decades for OU students and others who recirculated "Athens, Ohio." Bringing pastoral themes common to some Romantic literature to the hilly southeast Ohio landscape, the poem begins,

> Sweet Athens! The home of learning and beauty,
>
> How I long for thy hills and thy rich balmy air:
>
> For thy wide-spreading green, smiling sweetly on duty,
>
> And the valley beneath, and the stream winding there:
>
> On the north the high rock, on the south the lone ferry:
>
> The ville on the east, and the mill on the west .... (Emerson)

Notably, the first two ideas that Emerson associates with Athens are "learning and beauty." After this, he pays tribute to the town's natural surroundings as well as to events that facilitated student development, for sprinkled throughout are references to the university curriculum and the literary societies, including the "fun of blunders at each recitation!" (Emerson). However, more revealing is the fact that multiple Athenians published it before and after 1900, while the nationally influential William Rainey Harper, president of the University of Chicago, was delivering addresses predicting a bleak future for poorly funded postsecondary institutions (Diener 54). The timing and venues of the poem's reappearances hint at the poem's usefulness to OU members who were invested in upholding a flattering image of their institution and southeast Ohio despite rapid population and economic growth, as well as related increases in political clout, to the north and west. Moreover, in 1911, other locally focused creative writing by OU alumni circulated publically when OU history professor Clement L. Martzolff published William Dana Emerson's poem "To the Ohio River" and William Edward Gilmore's poem "Lines Written on Mount Logan" in a book of Ohio poetry. These poems join "Athens, Ohio," in emphasizing the natural beauty of southern and eastern Ohio.

On a basic level, the promotion of these writings as OU, Athens, and southeast Ohio fought state neglect show that the act of focusing attention can be kairotic, a tactic of recognizing the idea cluster OU-Athens-southeastern Ohio "among powerful strategic discourses" (McComiskey 113). Powerful discourses to which OU students responded included political, economic, and cultural perspectives that downplayed southeastern Ohio's interests when setting state priorities and remembering state achievements. And even though today we cannot know exactly how many people were influenced by locally focused OU student writing that circulated in the decades around 1900, we can sometimes see the writing's entry into local public awareness. For example, at OU's Columbiad Literary Society, which lasted from 1895 to 1901 and held its meetings in the home of an OU professor (at first Willis Boughton, later Edwin Watts Chubb), student members shared their writing with each other and with Athens residents such as the host professor (*The Columbiad* 1). Though the society concentrated on "purity of language, creative work, and the development of American literature" (*The Columbiad*), student members also shared writing about topics familiar to OU and Athens, Ohio, audiences. At a meeting on February 26, 1896, a date when the society's recorder kept unusually detailed notes, students read poems called "An Arbor," "Cascade Glen," "An Idol," "To Alma Mater," "In Memoriam &[?] in[?] Frieze," "To Dr. F. Cacker[?]," "Beta Theta Pi," "When Greek Meets Greek," and "To John Greenleaf Whittier," and a story installment titled "The Pedagogue" (*The Columbiad* 52). These titles hint at foci that the students found worthy of capturing in writing, including fraternity and sorority systems ("Beta Theta Pi" and "When Greek Meets Greek"); one's school, college, or university ("To Alma Mater"); and teaching or teachers ("The Pedagogue" and possibly "To Dr. F. Cacker[?]"). Of the remaining topics, "An Arbor" and "Cascade Glen," even if intended to be imaginative, likely reflected the wooded, hilly terrain around Athens. From sharing and discussing writing on these topics, students in attendance would have learned more about campus and non-campus life. Any non-student townspeople in attendance would have been exposed to descriptive accounts of university social life and nearby rural scenes and would have had time to respond and critique. Finally, professors and administrators

Chapter Three

(e.g., Edwin Watts Chubb, who became both) would have seen how students and others imbue nearby locations with meaning.

The tendency of some students to write the local, which was portrayed as a chain of interaction between OU students and Athens residents, carried over to graduate student Elizabeth Irene Smith's 1938 master's thesis on OU history. Both a primary source (a piece of pre-1950s student writing) and a secondary source (a history of OU that synthesizes earlier records), her thesis casts 1890s OU students as beholden to a town that supported the students when the university could not:

> Students were dependent upon the community for most of their social diversion. The school was small and was in and of the community, and the homes were freely open to students. After East and West wings [sections of the University] were withdrawn as dormitories all students, men and women lived in private homes in town until the women's dormitories came in about 1900 Frequent parties were held in the homes of friendly townspeople. (Smith 127)

Like many OU students from the 1800s, Smith views the everyday lives of OU students and other Athens residents as intertwined, such as when she argues, "[local] public opinion was an effective means of social control in the students' activities" (111).

A final point meriting attention about the student writing that I consider here is that some of it stemmed from the wishes or allowances of faculty members—a point that I discuss more fully in Chapter Four. That is, even if students initiated and executed regionally aware rhetorical acts in their newspapers, literary societies, and extracurricular creative writing, the writing that the students completed for academic credit, like Elizabeth Irene Smith's thesis, would have had to comply with the standards of faculty or other supervisors. So Smith's thesis as well as undergraduate student writing that followed academically approved writing modes like description and exposition both fulfilled academic expectations and exposed topics of special interest in southeast Ohio. One textbook that supported this dual purpose writing was *College Composition: A Brief Course*, written by three OU English department faculty members and published in 1943. The authors, who comprised half of the English department's full professors as of 1940 and 1950 (*Ohio University Bulletin, 1940-1941, 1950-1951*), taught students to look to their own community for inspiration and writing topics: "[the student] has only to open his eyes, for there is a world around him so full of interest and tragedy and comedy that he can see and hear enough to provide himself with more material than he could ever use" (Caskey,

Heidler, and Wray 4). Initially, the textbook reads as a practical application of Deweyian-Progressivism, which privileged experiential education and the role of the self in society. However, an additional possibility appears once we notice that the textbook authors focus their summaries and activities on a community that, while unnamed, bears a striking resemblance to Athens, Ohio. They encourage readers to describe the sight of students in raincoats hurrying to class in the springtime (4). The authors present a hypothetical scenario of college themes that an instructor would likely assign, such as "My Landlady" and "My First Walk Under the Elms" (6). They ask students to "conduct an investigation of [their] college surroundings" (41). Also, they suggest writing topics such as "A College Room" and "My Roommate" (41-42). In terms of weather, vegetation, and social climate, these topics reflect the environment of Athens, not, for example, much of the American West. Students in Athens would indeed have worn raincoats in the springtime and walked under American elms, and many students would have lived in quarters where they had landlords and roommates.

By the late 1940s, students were using common discursive modes to investigate local topics and activities, as evidenced in an honors first-year composition class's publication of a three-volume institutional history (discussed at length in Chapter Four): *Ohio University in the 1920s* (one volume) and *Ohio University in the Twentieth Century* (two volumes). To complete the descriptive or explanatory pieces filling these volumes, students researched print sources such as local newspapers and interviewed university authority figures to detail the social life of past OU students. One student wrote about selective student clubs such as a Folklore Club and a Booklover's Club, as well as regionally aware clubs such as the Rural Club, created for "students who were interested in rural life" (Hahnel). Another student commented on OU's nineteenth-century history, calling OU's first years bright and then observing that OU closed for three years in the 1840s due to "a lack of funds." This student continued, "In 1848, when [the university] reopened, many of the former students had gone elsewhere and enrollment was small; however, in the next few years it began expanding again although there was never enough money available for repairs and improvements" (Morris, "Introduction—1900"). Whether students such as these described local clubs for the purposes of documentation or defense, and whether the students reviewed moments of OU's past financial distress for the purpose of applying blame or commemorating institutional perseverance, the students, now several decades after 1900, were continuing a tradition of writing about events and activities that had shaped OU, Athens, and southeast Ohio. More than generating knowledge for knowledge's sake, many of the students and their mentors can be seen as striving to keep the work and needs of their institution visible and appreciated during a time when memories lingered of near invisibility.

Chapter Three

Despite the fact that most of the OU student writing that has been retained from the decades around 1900 was not overtly political in form or tone, and much of it sidestepped direct contributions to state-level political, economic, and cultural discussions, the writing can be understood in a context beyond that of the university alone and within that of a state whose centers of education, business, and industry were still emerging in the late nineteenth century. Furthermore, the tendency of OU students to bypass direct challenges to state-level discussions makes it all the more compelling as strategic counters to powerful discourses, for the writing shows how genres that were approved by institutional authority figures and perceived as generally apolitical can support local rhetorical engagement. Cases of college students in pre-1950s Houston further illuminate how apolitical-seeming genres can dress students' ideas in the vestments of academic legitimacy and, thus approved, render students' perspectives intelligible to wider audiences.

ADVOCATING A NEW KIND OF STUDENT IN HOUSTON

At UH and its community college predecessors, pre-1950s student writing fit a number of genres, and if studied apart from its relationship to the founding of Houston Junior College (HJC) and Houston Colored Junior College (HCJC), the student writing could be interpreted as exercises in perpetuating empty writing forms: the newspaper article, the descriptive essay, the research paper. Also, pre-1950s student writing at UH blurred lines between the nascent specialization area called composition and disciplines such as journalism, public speaking, theater, education, and creative writing. My argument here is that the genres and disciplines in which these students wrote reveal a strategy by which students completed college requirements while also entering local rhetorical exchanges. Genre and disciplinary location facilitated the writing's public work by letting students communicate their interests and expose, in academically approved ways, educational problems. As with historical OU writing, students from HJC and HCJC did not respond to one person and act in a single fleeting situation, as a speech-oriented version of kairos would demand, but wrote of their lives and shared their insider perspectives on education, especially higher education, to readers in a city that had no sizeable population of Houston-area public college students, no demographic of this type to reach, until the 1920s.

The most well-known interaction in Houston to which pre-1950s UH students responded was a mid-1920s discussion between leaders of the Houston Independent School District (HISD) and Houston high school students who lacked higher education opportunities unless they left the city or entered the private and selective Rice University. In 1926, approximately twelve high school students met with HISD Superintendent Oberholtzer to discuss the city's higher education limitations (Oberholtzer 19; Nicholson 10). Though no transcription remains from that meeting, local lore holds that it resulted in Oberholtzer's decision to open HJC and the supposedly separate but equal HCJC to prepare growing numbers of working students to enter civic and professional life. Nationally, public junior colleges in the 1920s were also responding to local needs (Witt et al. 107; Diener 9). As Witt et al. explain in their history of American junior and community colleges, "if the local factory needed welders, the junior college quickly produced a welding course. If local art lovers demanded cultural events, the junior college developed an arts series. If the public demanded flower arranging, the college hired a local florist" (107). In the same vein, high school students in 1926 Houston needed a college, so educational administrators created two. HJC opened in 1927 in the city's San Jacinto High School, which continued to hold high school classes during the day and began to hold classes for HJC in the evening. Until the late 1930s, HJC, like HCJC, had no campus of its own apart from the city's existing buildings and organizations. Supported entirely by tuition dollars, HJC borrowed classrooms from San Jacinto High School and two nearby Baptist churches, and several of the college's early faculty members and administrators worked for San Jacinto High School during the day. In 1928, HJC students described their institution as "a hopeful experiment" ("Junior College"), a depiction that would resurface in the following decades.

The importance of HJC students' backgrounds and experiences in shaping this educational "experiment" cannot be understated. Generally, HJC students held jobs in the city, could not attend Rice University, or could not easily move elsewhere to obtain a college education. According to a 1948 summary of Oberholtzer's views, "the University of Houston set out … to provide a broad curriculum in response to the changing needs of the community and society at large" (Patterson 11). This depiction of UH (at first HJC) as an answer to student demand reappears in a 1950 dissertation by a UH faculty member that begins, "The basic philosophy of the University of Houston, as revealed through its aims, emphasizes those educational services growing out of the individual and community educational needs of the citizens of the area" (Cochran 1). The dissertation's author, J. Chester Cochran, credits the idea for his institutional study to Oberholtzer, by that time president of UH (1), and Cochran attributes his access to primary historical documents to Oberholtzer and to Oberholtzer's assistant, Dr. W.W. Kemmerer (iii).

Beyond Oberholtzer, a vision for a public higher education institution geared to the practical and philosophical needs of working students persisted among other HJC supporters even after 1934, when HJC transitioned from a junior college to the University of Houston. In 1938, Hugh R. Cullen, a city philanthropist who donated land to establish a permanent campus for UH and, three blocks away, a permanent campus for the Houston College for Negroes (now Texas Southern University), said, "[UH] must always be a college for the working man and woman." He continued, "You see I have a warm spot in my heart for those boys and girls who have to get their education the hard way" (qtd. in Bolling 69). Given this justification, Cochran could report in 1950,

> Every phase of [UH] life is closely tied in with community affairs. Journalism students are on the Houston dailies, weeklies, and radio news service. The drama and music departments work in cooperation with Houston amateur and professional entertainment. Business courses are closely tied in with Houston firms, and are often taught by outstanding business authorities on a part time basis. Radio students do actual broadcasting work on professional stations. The whole aim of the university life is not of a cloistered academic nature, but rather of a living educational experience, brought about by close integration in community life. (43)

Cochran and other institutional figures from 1927 to 1950 did not single out particular writing courses to study relative to the desires that prompted the creation of HJC. However, the student writing that UH has retained from that period can be examined for how it supported college students' assertions of their identities and needs, underscoring and furthering the actions of the mid-1920s high school students who met with Superintendent Oberholtzer to discuss the city's non-existent public higher education options. If we view 1930s-1940s student writing from UH and its junior college predecessors as specific tactical moves (i.e., kairotic moves, in the sense used by McComiskey) to address Houston's late recognition of and support for public higher education, we see that students used academic or otherwise familiar writing genres to contribute to Houston-area discussions about the identity and needs of city residents like them. Although it was common in the early 1900s for junior colleges to contribute to community discussions (Diener 9), cases from 1930-1940s Houston draw attention to genres by which a hitherto absent public college student demographic could make inroads toward influencing civic discourse.

Today, three sources remain that feature numerous writings from Houston's public college students from 1927 to 1950. One of them, the student newspaper *The Cougar*, spans this entire period. A second source, an annual anthology called *The Harvest*, began in 1936 and showcased writing by HJC and later UH students who were enrolled in first-year composition and creative writing classes taught by Ruth Pennybacker. A third source, essays from 1930s-1940s seniors, illustrates advanced research-based student writing from the Houston College for Negroes, the HISD-governed successor to the Houston Colored Junior College. (In 1947, the Houston College for Negroes would change its name to Texas Southern University to reflect its newfound status as an independent public institution.) Through all of its years as HCJC (1927-1934) and through most of its years as the Houston College for Negroes (1934-1945), this institution operated out of Yates High School, a public African American school a few miles away from the HJC-based San Jacinto High School. Because *The Cougar*, the first of the three sources that I consider here, contains the only full-text pieces from numerous HJC students in the wake of HJC's founding, I focus on articles published from 1927 to the early 1930s, when the college was most visibly settling on an identity. In the case of my second source, *The Harvest*, I focus on two of the longest and most vivid essays in which students described and explained their educational experiences. Finally, in the case of my third source, senior essays from the Houston College for Negroes, I analyze two essays from the earliest years available (1936-37), essays that gave students a forum for responding to the social conditions of the surrounding region.

In the student newspaper *The Cougar*, many of the articles published in the late 1920s read as near copies of one another because they concentrate on HJC's rising prominence relative to older and better-known colleges and universities near and far. Histories of the college, details about the college's growth, and calls for increased school spirit appear across the issues, frequently accompanied by pictures of Oberholtzer (in fact, the same picture of Oberholtzer) and pictures of other administrators and faculty members. But despite the uniformity of many of the articles, perhaps even due to this streak of sameness, the articles accomplished the important rhetorical work of spotlighting merits of HJC students and an HJC education for a city populace that was unaccustomed to supporting a public higher education accessible to workers.

A slew of late-1920s articles promote HJC's milestones and early 1930s articles promote HJC students' achievements, and in both cases, the articles cover students' potential to contribute to civic affairs. In addition to keeping HJC students informed, the articles provide facts and ideas that any reader could begin to associate with the growing institution, facts and ideas that I see as strategic selections in light of the context of HJC's founding—boosterism to counter past higher education absences. In the early 1930s, many front-page articles touted the performance of HJC students during debate tournaments with other institutions and during plays organized by the College's Dramatic Club. Repeatedly, these articles emphasize the wins and other successes accumulated by HJC students, often compared to students from older and established institutions, as in the article titled "Debate Squad to Challenge Ten Colleges," centered on the front page of a 1933 issue. By the time of one March 1934 issue, the front page was dominated by articles titled, "H.J.C. Debates With Team from Tex. University," "Dramatic Club Staged Farce at the College," and "H.J.C. Debaters Against A&M in Debate." By October 1934, some of the articles lauded specific HJC faculty members for their personalities and teaching styles, as Chapter Two discussed. At this point, the writing worked like advertisements to entice prospective students to attend classes taught by the faculty. For the similar task of singling out and lauding HJC students, the newspaper published a front-page article in 1934 that identified the high schools that each HJC student had attended. Readers accustomed to skimming newspaper pages starting from the upper left-hand corner would have found this article first and then proceeded to articles on dancing, a student advisory board, a student assembly, and a meeting of the Dramatic Club.

In the student magazine *The Harvest*, HJC and later UH students wrote in an array of genres and modes—descriptions, narrations, poems, reviews, fiction, much of it on topics observed or otherwise experienced in the social surround. So in addition to pieces on topics as varied as Richard II and the Earth's past, students wrote descriptions and expositions on Houston scenes: working as a Houston bouncer, hitchhiking in Texas, witnessing a flood that damaged Houston. Beyond giving factual information about the city is the fact that many of these pieces, particularly those from the 1930s, conveyed details about the students' lives: their employment, their life prospects, the sites and activities that they knew. The Houston that comes across for public consumption is a Houston that public college students who had many non-academic responsibilities knew well. As Ruth Pennybacker, the publication's faculty sponsor, reported in her introduction to the first volume (1936), the students "write what interests them most" ("Part I" iv).

Personal essays that discuss education in relation to students' other obligations do particularly important work in *The Harvest* because they highlight struggles that these students faced, and they insist upon the value of accessible public higher education in the city. This is clearest in two of the longer essays: "College Deferred," by Hilda Long Lemon, published in 1938, and "I Live in America," by Albert Farias, published in 1941. In the former, Lemon identifies herself as a nontraditional student from a community where marriage and childrearing went unquestioned as a woman's top priorities. In response to a younger relative who called her "dumb" for taking thirty years to graduate from college after earning a high school diploma, Lemon details her return to education. She explains that during adulthood she resumed her reading, much of it out loud, in an attempt to favorably influence her unborn child—a caregiving approach that she discovered from her own reading (Lemon 1-2). After then describing her years spent as a wife and mother who participated in social events, Lemon presents her choice to return to college as a gesture of non-conformity. "I was always a misfit," she writes (2). Without female role models who had college degrees and without informing her family, she enrolled in college courses, an act that led her husband to question "the wisdom of her indulgence" (3).

Despite these hardships, Lemon describes her HJC and UH education in glowing terms. She writes that HJC "seemed more willing [than select institutions] to take a chance. It was new and inclined to concede the applicant the desire for an education" (3). She also refers to "certain new methods" that the General College of HJC wanted to explore, adding, "I enrolled there as the humblest of freshman, and it is not too much to say that we experimented together" (3). Reflecting on her college education as a whole, she writes,

> If we [students at HJC and later UH] have lacked the staunchness of noble trees under which to rest, we have had the strength of courageous educational leaders upon which to learn. If we have lacked the inspiration of tradition, we have shared the vision of pioneers. *Our administration officials are men who do not look upon educational problems as solved.* The Vice-President came to us once a week during the first two years to discuss these problems. As he stood before us frankly submitting his ideas and honestly seeking our reactions, we gained a comprehension of what to teach youth and how best to go about it. My son was of high school age. If I had learned nothing else, the *clearer understanding of the questions involved in his schooling* would be worth the effort of the past four years. (Lemon 4, emphasis added)

To Lemon, an activity whose value transcends generations and deserves appreciation is co-investigation from students and administrators into educational problems. This is among the activities that she uses to push back against derogatory generalizations about college students like her, people who did not enter college directly from high school and who neglected to accumulate great wealth.

Shedding light not on gender inequality as much as ethnic diversity is UH student Albert Farias in his 1941 essay, "I Live in America," in which he describes his childhood in rural Mexico and his eventual move to Houston with his mother and siblings (see Fig. 3). Besides explaining the strictness of his Mexican education and his later difficulties reading and writing in English, Farias discusses the concept of social class and its connection to education. After describing a marketplace scene that he remembers from Mexico, he comments, "I never knew what these poor people, the working class of Mexico, had in their minds

Chapter Three

that made them look so quiet and untalkative. They are the peons of Mexico who struggle under the lowest standard of living. Their education is low, and some cannot even write their own names" (20). Although Farias never names the

Figure 3. First Page of Albert Farias' "I Live in America," The Harvest, 1941. Courtesy of the Archives and Special Collections, University of Houston.

social class that he identifies with, we can infer a working class affiliation from his story of earning low wages in Mexico, then moderate wages in Houston, along with his need to provide for his mother.

To conclude his piece, Farias shares that he and his family "gradually began to become acquainted with the new customs and ways of living in Texas" and that in time he graduated as salutatorian of his high school class (23). Next for him came UH where he studied "Business Administration, Aviation and Education" (23). However, rather than end his essay by reflecting on his personal achievements, as might be expected of a college student writing about lived experiences and personal observations, he broadens his comments about education by reflecting on the relationship between education and cross-cultural interaction: "I think there is a strong need for Mexican teachers who know English to teach in Mexico in order to bring a closer understanding and unity among the Americans in this tragic time of world conflict. I think there might be a place there for me" (23). His push for unity during worldwide turmoil doubtlessly responds to conditions surrounding World War II, but the fact that Farias locates the push in relation to Mexico and to English speakers also acknowledges a nearby intercultural surround—precisely the kind of surround experienced by growing numbers of Houston residents seeking an education relevant for life in the greater Houston area, including its transnational links. If an Anglo-dominated Houston of the early 1940s saw UH producing workers for the city, Farias reminded them that the city's interests traverse linguistic and national borders, involving more people than some Houstonians realized. His essay joins Lemon's piece and the many HJC-centric newspaper articles to contribute to what McComiskey calls "the flow of cultural production" (117). Not subversive in form, and tied directly to English or journalism coursework, this body of student writing nonetheless stood to influence the city population's perception of Houston residents by virtue of appearing across classes, venues, and years.

Finally, if we remember that the Houston Independent School District (HISD) founded and governed UH's predecessor, HJC, at the same time that the HISD founded and governed HJC's African American counterpart, the Houston Colored Junior College, we avail ourselves of perspectives that reveal some of the educational needs of early African American college students in Houston. In 1934, the Houston Colored Junior College became the Houston College for Negroes, at which point its students could cap their four years of study with a research-based essay that needed approval from a faculty committee. From 1936 until the early 1940s, the English department of the Houston College for Negroes kept several senior students' essays, which addressed canonical literary topics and education topics. Generally, this writing encouraged appreciation of famous works of imaginative writing or called for improvements to

Chapter Three

learning opportunities for African American students in Texas. But regardless of whether the writing dwelt on texts or human subjects, it drew attention to a desired outcome of literacy education at the college: racial uplift. Below, I consider examples from the first two years of essays that have been retained (1936-37), a time period that set the tone for subsequent essays.

From 1936, there remains only one thesis, "An Enperiment [sic] in the Teaching of English in the Furney Richardson Rural High School of Teague, Texas, 1935-1936," by Christine G. Kelley Howard, whose argument supports a theme stretching across many of the 1937 essays: mastery of language increasing one's prospects of a successful life. Howard begins,

> Good speech is the power that brings success to all of man's activities, but this invaluable power is not yet a part of the fortune that fills the coffers of the Furney Richardson school community. Read with me if you will and watch our efforts, and the developments toward improving the conditions. After we have finished reading, give your suggestions for a more rapid progress. (1)

Not only does Howard link language education to one's life prospects, but she also invites readers to study her insights and offer suggestions. Even if intended only for academic readers, this research encourages those readers to apply empirical knowledge in the name of "rapid progress"; it supposes readers who are actively engaged in supporting educational reform at nearby schools. After then mentioning that she has worked for ten years in the Furney Richardson area in east Texas, between Dallas and Houston (1), Howard discusses educational strategies implemented in that school district, including gains made by African American high school students after the students began reading literary pieces written by other African Americans (2-3). Also, at one point she discusses a class's letter writing activity, explaining that the class's best student letter was mailed to actual recipients; the students then studied the letter's responses to examine different uses of punctuation (11). Here and in many of the other early HCN essays, mastery of surface features of language became a step toward giving marginalized students the type of resource discussed by David Gold in his study of Texas Woman's College—"access to the language of power" (Gold 89), a recurring point in critical pedagogical research (e.g., Delpit 282).

From the next year, 1937, nine senior essays remain, and they address literacy learning, the Psalms as literature, the life and poetry of Langston Hughes, periodicals by and for African Americans, Shakespeare's poems and plays, the African American poetic tradition, and sermons of African American ministers. For the first and most empirical of these essays, "A Survey of the English

Fundamentals Tests of the 1936 Seniors of the Houston College for Negroes," student Magdalene Clinton administered a test to study the writing of her fellow students at the Houston College for Negroes. Like Howard before her, Clinton emphasizes solutions to the data that she gathered: "Since we have learned that language is largely affected by environmental influence we have tried to note carefully the results and have attempted to offer suggestions for possible solution in order that these, or a large number of the common, ordinary, and frequent errors in both speaking and writing English may be eliminated" (20). While undoubtedly Clinton directed her paper to faculty members who would grade it, she nevertheless supposed that faculty members would want to act on her insights at that institutional site.

Additionally, Clinton even more than Howard asserts links between mastering correct written and spoken English (cause) and improving one's life and the standing of one's racial or ethnic group (effect). Through her citations, Clinton demonstrates familiarity with both the *English Journal* and Adams Sherman Hill's *The Principles of Rhetoric*, and like Howard, Clinton links correct language use to social and economic empowerment for African Americans. She connects nineteenth-century scholar George Herbert Palmer's comment, "Whoever goes to his grave with bad English in his mouth has no one to blame for the disagreeable taste except himself; for if faulty speech can be inherited, it can also be exterminated" (qtd. in Hill 17), to training that will produce "tomorrow's leader and citizen" (Clinton 21). Afterward, she connects a point from the *English Journal* about effective expression to her hope that "very soon the Negro race, especially the future leaders and members of social society, will have through the aid of conscientious teachers and will power to succeed, at least a fair command of this rich, expressive, and interesting language" (21). In the same vein, Clinton concludes by positing that the grammar and punctuation test that she administered to students as part of her study

> told [the students] where [they] needed to concentrate. In turn, the intelligent and thoughtful student who wanted to qualify for his place in life and at the same time give himself justice, did not stop his research and study until he was thoroughly familiar with the fundamentals of English in both writing and speaking. (23)

In Clinton's hands, perhaps as in the hands of many students educated at Houston College for Negroes, error correction and rule learning correlated to struggles for justice and enhanced quality of life. In other words, mastering formal rules of writing was viewed as a step to democratic participation and improved social status, an outlook similar to that of Professor Melvin Tolson at Wiley

College (Gold 59).

Once we recognize a version of kairos grounded in local response, collective involvement, and gradual change, we can begin tracking rhetorical action with sophistic ties in 1930s writing from African American students at the Houston College for Negroes and white students at Houston Junior College and the University of Houston. Directly or indirectly, across semesters or years, the student writing from these institutions countered a lack of public college student perspectives from Houston before the mid 1920s, and the writing championed new opportunities to educate the region's growing and diversifying body of workers and high school students. Also, contrary to what we might expect if using McComiskey's descriptor "subversive texts" (117), the students at these institutions wrote in forms that were well defined and presumably taught by faculty members, forms earning the students academic approval. As students upheld those forms—narratives, descriptions, empirical studies, newspaper articles—the students asserted their backgrounds and community needs. If students refrained from asserting their *personal* needs, as in the case of the earliest held student papers from the Houston College for Negroes, then the students selected people to study or discuss who resembled them, such as fellow African American college students in Houston. When viewed together, these very different pieces of writing across related institutions seem to say, repeatedly, *we are the growing population in Houston that needs public higher education, and here is why.*

ACADEMIC FORMS, PUBLIC ORIENTATIONS

If we view kairos less as thoughtfully timed utterances to single audiences than as strategic local responses to powerful discourses, we allow for some of the textual and organizational complexity that has characterized life for many students in American colleges and universities, institutions that in turn thrive, sustain, or decline for particular reasons. The Ohio and Houston, Texas, cases presented in this chapter show that whether one looks across several decades at a single institution or whether one looks across a few years at many connected institutions, one can ask, to whom—in addition to an instructor or college class—were students responding? What predated the student writing that might have mattered to the students given the historical texts that remain? Whether losing or acquiring people, assuming a marginal or central status, a geographical area's challenges permeate its public higher education institutions, and one manifestation of this influence is through student writing.

Furthermore, the cases from this chapter indicate that even the most formalized and academic of writing can help students respond to preexisting issues that they find persistently important. This is no small point given that it follows generations of historical scholarship indicating that instructors' and textbook writers' reliance on form, via genre, writing formulas, or the modes of discourse, risked shutting down students' rhetorical awareness. Most famously, Albert R. Kitzhaber, in his study of late-nineteenth-century rhetoric, argued,

> The effect of the forms of discourse [narration, description, exposition, argumentation, and sometimes persuasion] on rhetorical theory and practice has been bad. They represent an unrealistic view of the writing process, a view that assumes writing is done by formula and in a social vacuum. They turn the attention of both student and teacher toward an academic exercise instead of toward a meaningful act of communication in a social context. (139)

Kitzhaber's study of rhetoric manuals yielded numerous examples of form operating for form's sake. However, in the student writing that I consider above, newspapers articles, anthologies, literary societies, research essays, and the like, students engaged with their surrounding circumstances in spite of, maybe even *because* of, the academic or popular forms that their writing took. Whereas composition scholar Thomas M. Masters saw the late-1940s-era essay assignment as "neutralizing" first-year composition students' passion about their topics (169-70), I saw pre-1950s students at OU and UH writing in essay and other forms that could channel the students' observations and convictions toward the appearance of respectability for readers.

In his study of student writing at Texas Woman's University circa 1900, David Gold observes approvingly that TWU students wrote for their institutional newspapers and magazines; the only students who wrote traditional essays judged based on grammar and punctuation were students in TWU's remedial classes (92). I share Gold's approval of a range of writing forms, and I would add that even formulaic essay writing completed in class or for class credit can have rhetorical value beyond the classroom. To return to a view of kairos that centralizes specific, strategic language moves as they respond to powerful discourses, we are left with the question of how strategy pertains to the student writing that I consider above. Initially, the fact that OU and HISD-governed students wrote what they were taught hardly smacks of strategy (at least on the part of students). Yet I posit that the very familiarity of the writing forms used by students worked in the students' favor: students could expect readers, including readers from older generations, to recognize the writing forms as sanctioned by academe, part of the knowledge of higher education institutions to disseminate. Thus legitimized, the student writing would have a chance of being heard and deemed intelligible, seen as products of study. The topics that students address and the forms that their writing takes suggest an extra-academic current running underneath otherwise academic activity—academic work as public work. Mary Soliday has argued, "everyday school forms are (or could be) no less situated a writing practice than professional or workplace genres" (*Everyday Genres* 1). I would like to extend her position beyond comparisons of academic and professional writing by observing that we have a long way to go to understand and value the potential of familiar academic writing forms to help students reach audiences beyond college borders. If genre theorist Anis Bawarshi is right when he writes, "genres help organize and generate our social actions by rhetorically constituting the way we recognize the situations within which we function" (24-25), then historical OU and HISD-governed student writing in newspaper columns, poems, personal essays, senior essays, and so on can be valued for constituting students as learned, locally invested residents who, under the sponsorship of their higher education institution, could begin to refashion their relationship to community members.

Thus, one issue in play in the Ohio and Houston cases examined in this chapter is persuasion. Whereas college student writing in America between the Civil War and World War II has been associated with goals other than persuasion (Connors 49), early writing from OU and HISD-governed students persuaded via academically acceptable forms whose contents supported the interests of students and other university affiliates in a changing landscape or cityscape. Conceptualizing persuasion in this way does not disqualify present-day writing instructors from continuing to explore popular routes by which students enter and shape local arguments (e.g., Rivers and Weber). Instead, this perspective complements pedagogical initiatives grounded in public advocacy or service learning, highlighting the potential of even common academic writing modes, genres, and activities to shape students' public personas. Activist writing need not always take the form of manifestos, editorials, websites, or pamphlets, this research shows. Kelly Ritter arrived at a similar point when studying a post-World War II women's college anthology called the *Yearling*, which featured writing ranging from the creative to the expository. She notes that although she was not surprised that students submitted writing from many genres to the *Yearling*, she was surprised "that the chosen content was often quite compelling and current" (*To Know* 69) Further work remains to be done to understand what is uniquely advantageous about creative and other indirectly persuasive writing that fosters kairotic action by enabling students to speak back to regulatory conditions in their surroundings.

Tracking a kairotic sensibility in historical college student writing, while another way to locate the writing, stops short of preparing scholars to show how student writing has related to all other people and interests. Like an analysis of institutional nomoi, it peels back one more layer of the writing's spatial work.

However, the larger process of building on sophistic outlooks on situated meaning, whether through nomos, kairos, or another concept, lets scholars and instructors specify how, and with what significance, student writing interacts with places. Continuing the process in Chapter Four, I examine the relationship between student writing and institutional campaigns to display student excellence to other higher education institutions. It is important to remember that when student writing was aimed at readers beyond campus borders, the writing could encounter members of other colleges and universities—or at least readers who carried with them perceptions of other colleges and universities. And before the 1950s, as today, perception mattered. So, complicating clean academic-public binaries, I consider this complex chain of interactions.

CHAPTER FOUR
COMPOSITION ON DISPLAY: STUDENTS PERFORMING COLLEGE COMPETENCE

By broadening institutional expectations for student behavior and reminding readers of underrepresented places and people, pre-1950s student writing at OU and UH did significant rhetorical work. But lest I shut down opportunities to further unpack spatial dimensions of student writing, I continue to endorse *dissoi logoi*, literally meaning opposing words or arguments, but perhaps better explained as "a means of discovering *a* truth" rather than *the* truth (Jarratt, *Rereading* 49). Too, I heed philosophy scholar Christopher W. Tindale's explanation that *dissoi logoi* does not mean that one takes all sides of an idea to be equally true, but that the one shows how multiple sides can be taken and then, with that knowledge, how to take the side that one finds most prudent (103). At issue is how one acts after one considers multiple perspectives, a point taken up by Susan C. Jarratt when, in an analysis of Plato's *Theaetetus*, she argues that because every idea can be understood differently, what matters is to negotiate "action for groups of people given their varying perceptions of the world" (*Rereading* 50). For my project, action belongs to the reader of this book given the conditions (e.g., type of institution, kind of historical texts available, time to devote to historical research) experienced by the reader and that make any one of my analyses of historical student writing more applicable than the others to the reader's location. Thus, to some but not all readers, this chapter may provide the most useful way to analyze student writing at some institutions, but neither this chapter nor the surrounding chapters pretends to illustrate all of the spatially nuanced rhetorical work of student writing.

In this chapter I examine another interaction that weaves through historical records at OU and UH: the interaction between early student writing itself and displays of the writing targeting audiences on and off campus. Whereas in Chapter Three I showed that pre-1950s OU and HISD-governed students engaged public issues by writing in innocuous academic genres, I now consider how student writing supported *other* people's arguments—campus leaders' campaigns to portray academic excellence to audiences near and far. Through their involvement with and presentation of student writing, campus leaders such as administrators and influential faculty members favorably compared students at

Chapter Four

their institution to students at other postsecondary institutions, and in effect, the leaders re-presented the value of their institution's students. From this angle, writing that bears students' names can be seen as carefully packaged products that non-students held up for outside acclaim, a situation reminiscent of the epideictic tradition.

Today, epideictic language is usually associated with Aristotle and equated with speeches whose primary purpose is to praise or blame, or, more generally, equated with ceremonial language used to portray a topic positively or negatively. However, I want to consider an earlier, more provocative version of epideixis grounded in First Sophistic sensibilities and discuss how this version can help us situate college student writing in relation to its surroundings. We glimpse some effects of specific sophists' epideixeis in Hippias of Elis' remark that he "made a great reputation" in Sparta by "discoursing on noble pursuits that a young man should follow," followed by his comment about his lecture's popularity in Sparta and probable popularity in Athens (Plato, "*Hippias Major* 286A"). The stress that Hippias' places on his range of knowledge also appears when he says, "I ... always go up from my home in Elis to the congress of the Greeks at Olympia at the time of the festival, and also submit myself to the sacred precinct to speak on whatever subject anyone may choose from those that I have prepared for a display, and to answer whatever questions anyone may wish to ask." After then mentioning Socrates, Hippias—as described by Plato—adds, "For never, since I began to compete at Olympia, have I met anyone superior to myself in anything" (Plato, "*Hippias Minor* 363C-D, 364A"). Regarding other sophists, we glimpse comparable effects in Socrates' announcement, "Our comrade Prodicus here [a sophist] has often in the past come to visit in a public capacity; but just recently, when he came here from Ceos on public business, he gained the greatest renown, both in speaking before the council and in giving private lectures" (Plato, "*Hippias Major* 282C"). As these examples suggest, the desired outcomes of some sophists' epideixeis began with an enhancement of their public image so that they could attract wider audiences.

Additionally, the early sophists' epideictic tradition rested on the idea that the ornate, self-aware language of theater reminded audiences of language's constructed qualities, and that even so, theatrical language produced effects capable of changing perception and spurring action. This outlook contrasted the notion that language primarily transmits consensually held facts (what present-day compositionists would call transactional rhetoric). As obvious as the sophistic perspective seems when applied to *theater*, certain sophists also applied it to domains of human activity outside of theater, domains such as the court. John Poulakos explains,

> When the sophists converged on Athens, the most accomplished form of spectacle was the drama of the theater. As in

the case of competition, this institutionalized form of cultural activity shaped sophistical rhetoric in its image, making public discourse a matter of performance and exhibition. In turn, sophistical rhetoric took exhibition outside the boundaries of the theater and into the forums of legal and political speaking. In so doing, it helped create the awareness that words do more than call forth the world the way poetry had done; they also create it, display it, and exaggerate some of its features and understate others. In other words, words are not only instruments of representation or vehicles of meaning but also actions performed on stages of their own making. (*Sophistical* 39)

Poulakos' account privileges the concepts of exhibition, or a publically oriented demonstration of selected language moves, and spectacle, or a representation that is consciously crafted from exaggeration and understatement. Both concepts carried over from theater to the domains of law and politics, and I would add that the concepts help us discern another layer of the rhetorical work of early-twentieth-century college student writing. Poulakos explains the ancient carryover from theater to law as "expand[ing] the field of the spectacular from the theater to the courtroom" and as "theatricaliz[ing] rhetorical discourse" (*Sophistical* 43). Likewise, via the concepts of exhibition and spectacle, I see movements to publicize college student writing before the 1950s as theatricalizing the writing, and I argue that this perspective has significance despite whether the people involved in publicizing the writing viewed their work in sophistic terms.

According to Bruce McComiskey, First Sophistic perspectives on epideictic language should be updated if they are applied to a contemporary context characterized by intertextuality and competing interests. Building on James Berlin's and Takis Poulakos' work on social class, he argues that today, "Epideictic oratory ... represents, always in political language, *perceived* values; and rhetors of any cultural group have the potential, realized or not, to represent social values as they perceive them, whatever the *status quo*" (91). McComiskey terms the resulting possibilities for discourse *graffitic immemorial, graffitic* because they lean on sociocultural context for meaning and *immemorial* because they re-present what has been repressed or excluded by earlier, dominant representations (93). For example, he mentions bumper sticker parodies of dominant cultural symbols, parodies that gain meaning by building on previous debates and discussions (graffitic) and that expose the perspectives of those seeking to challenge the status quo (immemorial). Although in the remainder of this chapter I examine collections of pre-1950s student writing at OU and UH, not a bumper sticker or a slogan from the digital age, I too analyze the growth

Chapter Four

of texts (student writing) within a context that was evolving as it introduced audiences to new perceptions of students and places. Furthermore, my analysis heeds the sophistic amalgamation of theatrical and non-theatrical discourses, the tradition of creating memorable public impressions by emphasizing and deemphasizing carefully selected points.

Here I track how institutional leaders at OU and UH used student writing from writing classes to promote an image of the leaders' institutions and students that leaders directed largely to off-campus audiences. At OU, late-1940s faculty and administrators collaborated to support and present a class of first-year composition students' writing, creating a public statement about the potential and accomplishments of first-year students at this institution. At UH, faculty members and administrators collaborated from 1936 to 1950 (and beyond) in a remarkably similar fashion when they worked with students to produce their institution's first literary magazine, *The Harvest*, which displayed a range of communication skills attributed to the students. Student writing supporting institutional public relations, we might call these two institutional cases. While I am unable to identify the primary reader or group of readers targeted by each of these collections of student writing, I can, if tracking endorsements and other contributions to the writing, show that non-students turned the writing into spectacles designed to impress readers other than students.

FIRST-YEAR OU STUDENTS AS SCHOLARS

The OU student writing that I examine in this chapter appeared in three volumes, *Ohio University in the 1920s: A Social History* (one volume) and *Ohio University in the Twentieth Century: A Fifty-Year History* (two volumes), all of which were published in 1950. The essays that filled each of the volumes were presented as the work of students from a 1949 honors first-year composition course taught by English professor Paul Kendall; however, closer analysis shows that non-students (faculty, staff, and administrators) influenced the essays' presentation and content. As I review these writings, I argue that they did more than describe early twentieth-century Ohio University. The writings presented OU in terms that compared it favorably to a higher education found elsewhere, thereby creating a public statement about the quality of OU students. Positive depictions of OU and its students appear most saliently in the front matter of the three volumes, so it is significant that for the two volumes after *Ohio University in the 1920s: A Social History*, an OU president penned an introductory note. After I examine the front matter, I look at the student essays themselves to see how influences from faculty, staff, and administrators shaped the perspective given of OU.

Ohio University in the 1920s: A Social History contains two consecutive introductions, the first introduction written by student Mary Lou Drum and focusing on 1920, the second introduction written by student Kathryn Morris and focusing on 1929. Drum says nothing about the purpose of the volume, but her focus reveals an interest in showing how OU had grown from 1920 to 1950. For example, she begins her introduction with a comparison: "Ohio University in 1920 was very much smaller and less complex than it is today. In curricula, faculty, student body, cost, and facilities Ohio University has grown immensely." The comparative focus strengthens in the next introduction, by Morris, who associates growth with the idea of importance. Morris begins, "The change in the appearance of the Ohio University campus and in the school itself between the years 1920 and 1930 all indicated growth and the increasing importance of Ohio University among the universities of the country." In her concluding paragraph, Morris begins, "In 1920 Ohio University was a small insignificant college which existed principally for the training of teachers; by 1929 it had grown in many ways." After then giving examples, Morris leaves readers with the comment, "In general everything seemed to point to the fact that Ohio University was rapidly becoming a school which might be compared favorably with any of the better universities of our state" ("Introduction—1929"). If readers opened *Ohio University in the 1920s: A Social History* with the hope of acquiring details about 1920s learning and campus activities, then before reaching those details, readers encountered introductions that emphasized growth, tied growth to betterment, and positioned OU as rising in prominence compared to other universities in the state or country. While brief, these moments recall the image-enhancing comparisons of the sophist Hippias and keep readers' attention on the proposed value, not just the factual descriptions, of Ohio University.

The tendency to associate student writing with public statements about academic excellence only intensifies in an introductory note written by OU President John C. Baker and appearing before a student-written introduction in the next two volumes, *Ohio University in the Twentieth Century: A Fifty-Year History*. Baker writes,

> Many favorable comments were made about the first manuscript [Ohio University in the 1920s], and it is believed this second document will have even wider appeal. These studies are excellent examples of the latent ability in student groups if their efforts are properly directed and stimulated. Both Professor Kendall and his students deserve the thanks of the University for the tremendous amount of work they devoted to this project and the scholarly and effective way in which

Chapter Four

they presented their material. (1)

The president's evocation of consensus—"Many favorable comments *were made,*" "it *is believed*" (emphasis added)—does not clarify the individuals who championed the student writing and does not specify what about the writing elicited positive reactions. But it does convey an idea of all-encompassing support, tying him and OU as a whole to the writings. Baker also reveals a connection between the student writing and someone else's standards when he says, "if [the students'] efforts are properly directed and stimulated" and "the scholarly and effective way in which [the students] presented their material." If the students' abilities were "properly directed," as President Baker claims, and if the students' writing was indeed "scholarly," then he implies that the goal of effective student preparation was for students to write like scholars, a goal that his institution could be seen as achieving. Despite whether the student writing in these volumes was originally intended to fulfill course requirements, the writing now formed part of a larger display of student achievement and institutional value, a display likely to interest readers capable of steering higher education institutions toward future prominence.

On a separate and subsequent page, accompanying idea associations are used to frame volume one of *Ohio University in the Twentieth Century: A Fifty-Year History* when a passage is quoted from English writer John Masefield's poem "A University, Splendid Beautiful and Enduring." The passage contrasts ominous forces such as "broken frontiers and collapsing values" with a university that "stands and shines; wherever it exists, the free minds of men urged on to full and fair inquiry, may still bring wisdom into human affairs." Thus ends the quoted segment, encouraging readers to see "a university," presumably Ohio University, as the force that "urge[s] on to full and fair inquiry" the minds of students (qtd. in *Ohio University in the Twentieth Century* 1). However, as the volume's student-attributed essays show, "full and fair inquiry" comes to resemble inquiry that supports faculty and administrators' visions of OU history, an echo of McComiskey's point that "epideictic oratory [or more broadly, epideictic rhetoric] … represents, always in political language, *perceived* values" (91).

While not all of the pieces attributed to students in the three-volume history of OU draw heavily from the opinions or words of faculty and administrators, the tendency as the volumes proceed is for students to use personal interviews with faculty and administrators to confirm what really happened in OU's recent past. The tendency is least pronounced in the first volume, *Ohio University in the 1920s: A Social History*, which includes a few citations from faculty; there, students rely far more heavily on student newspapers for support. However, after the apparent success of *Ohio University in the 1920s: A Social History* (Baker), students regularly mix personal interviews with print sources, and some of the students lean decidedly on personal interviews. What then occurs helps us to see the essays as tools with which non-students promoted a strategic vision of OU: 1) students give information from faculty and administrators without expressing reservations about the information's veracity, and 2) sometimes, by placing attributive tags in footnotes at the end of paragraphs, students neglect to specify exactly how much information comes from them and how much information comes from their sources (faculty and administrators).

Kathryn Morris' introduction to *Ohio University in the Twentieth Century: A Fifty-Year History* (volume one) eventually leans in this direction, providing a mild version of the influences that I describe above. After citing an early catalog, the Athens Board of Trade, an institutional history by OU history professor Clement L. Martzolff, and a student newspaper, Morris reaches her penultimate paragraph, whose main idea and most important language come from Dean Edwin Watts Chubb. The full paragraph reads,

> The college [OU] was so small in 1900 that the faculty-student relationship was much closer than it is today. This feeling was very important because as Edwin Watts Chubb, Dean Emeritus of the College of Arts and Sciences, has said, "A Great deal of the success of a university depends on the harmony between faculty members, between students, and between the faculty and students." (Morris, "Introduction—1900")

At the end of the paragraph is a footnote reading "Personal interview." In this example, the paragraph is brief, and quotation marks appear around the cited administrator's words. I share the paragraph because it is Dean Chubb's wisdom about the ingredients needed to create university harmony that allows Morris to convey the significance of 1900-era closeness between faculty and students. In a sense, Chubb's contribution allows the student to turn a single observation (which might have also come from Chubb) into a paragraph. However, many of the student writers whose essays follow Morris' introduction rely more extensively on ideas or language from institutional leaders, at times blurring boundaries between the students' contributions and faculty and administrators' contributions.

We begin to gain a wider view of the indebtedness of students in *Ohio University in the Twentieth Century: A Fifty-Year History* to faculty when noticing that in addition to taking a key analytical point from Dean Chubb, Kathryn Morris quotes Professor Martzolff as saying that one early 1900s OU president "ushered in the Greater Ohio University" (qtd. in Morris, "Introduction—1900")—no small claim. In a nearby piece about student clubs, another student recognizes

English professor Hiram R. Wilson for providing information about the founding of a student organization called the Booklover's Club. Later in this piece, the student acknowledges, in the essay proper and in a footnote, English professor Clinton N. MacKinnon's work to organize an honorary fraternity (Scott). Then another student mentions a recitation from Professor Paul Kendall at a play produced by the Ohio University Theatre (M. Anderson), adding no mention of the fact that Kendall was overseeing this student's writing and the writing of her peers. The possibility that these faculty members misremembered events or shared information selectively, much like the possibility that other kinds of sources could portray a university event in a different light, goes unacknowledged. The essays function as if the words of then current faculty members amount to consensually held truth.

More arresting, of course, is the tendency of faculty and administrators to contribute analysis or commentary as opposed to historical detail, as in the previously cited introduction of student Kathryn Morris. In *Ohio University in the Twentieth Century: A Fifty-Year History*, student Shannon Meeker incorporates faculty contributions of this kind when, spanning four paragraphs near the end of her essay "Campus Politics," she shares detailed comments from interviews that she conducted with two deans, one assistant dean, and an English professor—in contrast to a shorter version of this essay which appeared in *Ohio University in the 1920s: A Social History* and which lacked interview-based support. The institutional authority figures provide concluding, analytical comments about what campus politics means as well as prescriptions about what it should mean for students in 1950. For example, the dean of the University College is quoted as saying, "Despite the fact that the political campaigns on the campus sometimes result in a loss of noon hours and class time, students at Ohio University ought to take an earlier interest in politics. Furthermore, students should learn that politics are as they are, but should, however, desire and strive to improve them" (Starcher qtd. in Meeker). Meeker provides little analysis of her own concerning the four outside perspectives, merely reporting that her interviewees "have their variances of opinion" about the role of politics on campus. This essay and others reveal a theme of administrators and faculty members not only supporting but also guiding writing that was attributed to students.

The effect of incorporating institutional authority figures' analyses into a student essay can be felt more forcibly in the following piece, "Special Days and Celebrations," by Jean Davidson, a piece which reveals insight into the attitudes—the very mindsets—of earlier generations of faculty and administrators. Writing about a pre-1920s celebration called University Day and held in Athens by and for university members, Davidson describes the celebration's events, which included a parade, and then discusses the celebration's meaning to different university insiders. She ends one paragraph with a footnote that reads, simply, "Professor Clinton C MacKinnon, Professor of English," a paragraph that is as follows:

> Such a parade, as might be expected, was quite a spectacle for not only did it stretch endlessly around the town, but also it [sic] participants—*bored* college students and *begrudging* professors, sprinkled here and there with *a few who enjoyed the celebration* to the extent of wearing fancy dress in it—added to its hilarity. *Certainly this parade did not suggest the scholarly achievement befitting a university. Its death with the change of university presidents was no doubt a relief to all concerned.* (Davidson, emphasis added)

Here as in other passages, faculty names appear at the bottom of the page while information with which the faculty members are associated conveys nuanced sentiments that most first-year composition students from 1949-1950 could not have felt firsthand. Students could have researched earlier newspaper articles and other campus records to pinpoint dates, stated purposes, and perhaps general or isolated reactions to campus events. (Davidson's earlier citations indicate that she did so.) But it would have been quite another feat for a first-year composition student from 1949-1950 to describe the various feelings of people who attended a pre-1920s event and then unpack the event's significance in comparison to university standards from that time period.

Moments of ambiguous faculty contributions scarcely appear in the first of the three volumes of OU student writing. By *Ohio University in the Twentieth Century: A Fifty-Year History*, which broadens the time period covered by four decades, the students write longer pieces and faculty and administrator knowledge takes more central roles. Something of a push-pull surfaces, then, between students who write more as the volumes progress and faculty members who demonstrate more ways to shape the volumes as a whole. Based on these three volumes, the evolution of faculty influence at OU was not offset by moves from students to document sources, and faculty and administrators who wished to advance a certain perspective and interpretation of OU's achievements could do so. Faculty and administrator contributions gained importance by their placement and recurring appearance in the volumes, not unlike the selective emphasis that characterized the early sophists' theatrically informed epideixeis. Readers could be told that OU students write in a scholarly way (Baker), and faculty and administrators could uphold that vision by strengthening students' historical information and accompanying analyses. Though the student essays in these three volumes, particularly the final two volumes, extended an institutional portrait begun by Professor Kendall and university leaders, the essays reinforced rather than re-represented that portrait. In other words, the student essays were *graffitic* but not *immemorial*.

CREATIVELY COMPETITIVE STUDENTS AT UH

Founded in 1936, *The Harvest* was an annual magazine featuring UH student writing from the creative to the modal, at first student writing from Professor Ruth Pennybacker's creative writing and first-year composition classes. Here I consider the growth of the magazine from 1936 to 1950, and I examine how people other than students framed the magazine's writing so as to craft a public statement—which in turn evolved—about UH's writing programs and students. Especially through the magazine's front matter and editorial contributions, faculty and administrators exhibited an image of diverse students who, because of their backgrounds, were transforming UH into a writing hub worthy of widespread acclaim in and beyond academe.

Until the early 1940s, *The Harvest* was overseen by Ruth Pennybacker, whose doctoral work had been in literature and who went on to teach first-year composition and become associated with creative writing. The magazine's early issues name Pennybacker as their faculty sponsor, and in her introductions, Pennybacker endowed these issues with many layers of meaning. In Part I of the inaugural (1936) issue, she made the following points: impressive student writing comes from first-year, not only advanced, students; her writing classes accommodate students' various interests and ways of learning; she encourages students to produce writing that fits specific genres (arguably a contradiction of the previous point); and UH students are standouts, not like students found elsewhere. In fuller detail, she posits:

- Most of the magazine's writing (prose and poetry, imaginative work and informative pieces) "are by Freshmen and Sophomores of the General College of the University of Houston," with creative writing students contributing the bulk of the writing in Part I of issue one and other students producing the bulk of the writing in Part II of issue one.
- The student contributors write in flexible environments. Her courses have optional attendance, and "no definite assignments are made; the [students] write what interests them most." For this, she thanks UH, naming two upper-level administrators who let her "teach a writing class in an experimental way."
- She wants her students to produce "dramatic and literary reviews" because she believes that "the ability to criticize dispassionately is lacking

in many Americans and should be cultivated."
- She has "great faith in the type of student that the University is attracting," students who she says "are capable of unusual work." Some of the students contributed to the typing, illustrations, and editorial work of the first issue. ("Part I," 1: iv)

Stressing pedagogical flexibility, faculty influence, and a range of students, each one unique, Pennybacker establishes a starting point from which to frame UH students and the students' writing.

In Part II of the first issue, Pennybacker provides another introduction, now elaborating on her point about the unique and diverse student population and using this point to defend the value of teaching first-year composition at UH—a defense implying that her experiences are more positive than the experiences of writing instructors elsewhere. After adding that Part II features "twelve authors" who took her first-year composition class, at that time called Freshman English or Freshman Composition, she writes,

> I have never been able to understand why many instructors consider the teaching of Freshman Composition drudgery, and many students find it dull. Each of my thirty-eight Freshmen [the total number of Freshman English students whom she taught that year] has at some point turned in an interesting paper. Often their sketches reveal some significant fact about the writer's temperament, background, or literary ability. (Pennybacker, "Part II" 1)

Next, Pennybacker supposes that the fact that many of her students work to support themselves renders the students' "experiences too actual for their opinions to be cast in any mold" (ibid). She concludes, "Teaching them has been an enlivening experience" (ibid). One effect of this introduction is that readers were directed away from doubts that they may have had about the writing abilities of first-year composition students, and the readers were encouraged to see the students' nonacademic backgrounds as raw material with which the students enriched their writing. That is, Pennybacker's display of her students inches toward the early sophistic interest in spectacle, as Poulakos describes it (*Sophistical* 39), by including words that accentuate some features of her students or their writing ("enlivening," "interesting") and by downplaying the applicability of other available terms to her classes ("dull," "drudgery"). She suggests that although her students took classes at night because many of them worked during the daytime, what is most important for her readers to remember is that her students' experiences add value to their writing.

In her introduction to the following year's issue (1937), Pennybacker adds

Chapter Four

two explanations:
- When discussing the creative writing classes that she teaches, she not only shares that her students write what interests them, but also notes that "some [students] take the course for credit; others do not. The latter attend when they like and write as much as they like."
- When commenting on the diversity of her students, she not only claims that her students are capable of good work. Now she explains that the students' "actual contact with life ... makes them less conventional-minded than the average college person. They are individuals, not types." (Pennybacker, "Introductory Note," *The Harvest* 2)

A comparison of the first two issues of *The Harvest* shows that by the second issue, Pennybacker allows students to attend her classes despite the students' intention or ability to obtain college credit; in 1937 she highlights a spectrum of learning options that were not touted a year earlier. Also, from issue one (1936) to issue two (1937), Pennybacker goes from calling attention to her students' "unusual" abilities to, more specifically, praising her students' transcendence of conventions that control "the average college person." This added comparison of her students to "the average college person" is noteworthy, for comparisons to college students at other institutions appear more forcibly in later issues. UH students were not simply hard working and creative, the idea went; they were *more* hard working and creative than other college students.

In 1938, Pennybacker's point about the diversity of her students had also expanded, now filling a thick paragraph in which she observed that her students "hail from various parts of the world," come from "different racial and social groups," work in various capacities, and demonstrate an ability to share experience-based information on any topic, "from wheat-harvesting in Nebraska to mourning customs in France" (Pennybacker, "Introductory," *The Harvest* 3). To conclude this description, she writes, with bolder praise than she had used earlier, "Teaching [at UH] has been one of the broadest educational experiences I have ever had" (ibid). By 1939, she describes her students as entirely from her creative writing class (which was not the case every year), yet she nonetheless shares that her students include "a social worker, a broker's secretary, an artist, a real estate salesman, a nurse, and men employed by the oil refineries, in addition to the regular full-time students" (Pennybacker, "Introductory," *The Harvest* 4). This information would not have been news to her students, but it would have been news to readers who, using other colleges and universities as their benchmark, perceived college students as a single type of person.

In addition to crafting an ever more elaborate picture of UH students as diverse and hard working, the presence of administrative guides and supporters grew in and after 1939, a change that encourages readers to see *The Harvest* as representing UH as a whole and not one group of students. One sign of this comes when, in 1939, Pennybacker increased the number of administrators whom she thanked from two to three, one of the three a dean and another of them an assistant to the president. Then, in 1941, the front matter of *The Harvest* featured an additional page that listed numerous people involved in that year's issue. Here appears the announcement "Sponsored by the English Department of the University of Houston," with thirteen people, including Pennybacker and one of the administrators whom she had thanked in previous issues, listed underneath ("The 1941 Harvest," 6: ii). After this is the heading "Editorial Board" with Ruth Pennybacker listed as editor-in-chief, four other people listed as assistant or associate editors, and one person listed as the art editor (ibid). Pennybacker again wrote the 1941 issue's introduction, but now her institutional status changes from faculty member to administrator because her title by this point is "Chairman [sic] of the English Department" (Pennybacker, "Introductory," *The Harvest* 6). Whatever influence she then exerted would be associated with her job as a department administrator. Yet another sign of growing administrative influence over the 1941 *Harvest* is that, for the first time, Pennybacker thanks entire campus departments by name: the Department of Fine Arts and the Department of English. She thanks Fine Arts for providing an entire class of student illustrators (nineteen people in all) to help. About the English department, she writes, "The Harvest [sic] could never have attained its representative character without the loyal working together of the whole English department. The Editorial Board has spent a good many week-ends reading, assembling, and proof-reading material" (ibid). Thus, the student writing published in *The Harvest* by 1941 carried with it a stamp of approval associated with the UH English department and with selected upper-level administrators. The publication's image had changed so that *The Harvest* more obviously represented the "perceived values" (McComiskey 91) of an institution, giving us reason to suppose that the publication could have been renamed *The University of Houston Presents the Harvest*.

If the appearance of endorsements from entire departments failed to portray 1941 UH students as the diverse, compelling individuals that Pennybacker and UH leaders thought them to be, a new section in the back matter, "About the Authors," created another opportunity to publicize the students' varied backgrounds. Here readers could find biographical sketches of each student whose writing was featured, the sketches mentioning where the writers had lived (e.g., Tulsa, Oklahoma; Houston and Galveston, Texas; Zacapu, Mexico) and what the writers had experienced (e.g., marriage, service in the U.S. Navy, employment in a local shoe store, employment as a laboratory custodian). If readers had previously doubted Pennybacker's comments about the range of her students' experiences, the readers could turn to this section to find support for her claims.

The year 1942 marks a turn for *The Harvest* because Pennybacker went on a sabbatical, and a UH student assumed the position of editor-in-chief and wrote the issue's introduction. However, lest these changes lead us to conclude that students took control of the magazine, we should consider the 1942 students' hope to meet Pennybacker's standards: "Miss Pennybacker has in the past six years set a standard of excellence for **The Harvest** which this year's student board has worked to maintain" (Hicks et al.). More importantly, faculty and administrators enhanced their surveillance of *The Harvest* between 1942 and 1950. The year 1942 saw the formation of a "student editorial board" that would be "assisted by a faculty advisory committee" of three people (ibid). Where there was once one named faculty advisor, there were now three. And by 1946 there appeared a panel of judges comprised of faculty members to whom students should send their submissions for publication consideration ("Preface," *The Harvest* 11). The following year, Ruth Pennybacker, now with experience as a department administrator, returned to sponsor the magazine and join other faculty in judging the submissions ("Preface,' *The Harvest* 12). So even though issues from this time period listed students as authors of the introductions, new forms of oversight circumscribed the students' influence.

Two other changes in the front matter from 1942 to 1950 indicate how influences from students, faculty, and administrators converged. First, the issues made stronger comparisons of UH students both to one another and to students from other institutions. Second, the issues showed awareness of the effects of UH student writing during wartime suffering. If examined for what these new developments display for public consumption and what, through selective emphasis and de-emphasis, the developments make into a spectacle, we find much to consider. If any definite argument can be extrapolated from the front matter of the 1942-1950 issues, it is that UH students and their writing can and should impress audiences outside of UH and the Houston area. Concerning comparisons of UH students to competition within and beyond UH, issues from the mid and late 1940s frame student writing in terms of writing contests; increasingly, the writing published by *The Harvest* was writing that faculty judges had already deemed winners. The preface of the 1946 issue lists two winners of a short story contest and three winners of a poetry contest (one of whom, Vassar Miller, would later acquire a national reputation) ("Preface," *The Harvest* 11). The prefaces of the 1947 and 1948 issues mention a "Harvest Contest" that involved a panel of faculty judges. If before 1946 some of the students' contributions had been deemed winners of a contest, then that information would have been less apparent, located in the back matter as opposed to the front matter. Also, in the 1948 issue, UH student writing was discussed in terms that framed it in relation to student writing from other sites. The introduction from that year states, "We believe it our duty to call attention to the growing excellence in writing at the school. Our vision is to make the University the hub of the literary and intellectual wheel of the Southwest" ("Preface," *The Harvest* 13). Following this announcement of a regional "vision" for UH, a new paragraph begins with students thanking the president's assistant for his "encouragement and financial arrangements through the University Book Store" (ibid). Given its source of financial backing and its expression of UH's value via a regional academic hierarchy, *The Harvest* was operating as a marker of success, a platform from which students, faculty, and administrators could build a case for institutional excellence. Although more multifaceted a case than the speech of an individual sophist like Prodicus, who "gained the greatest renown" through his language (Plato, "*Hippias Major* 282C"), *The Harvest* of the late 1940s reveals that a step students, faculty, and administrators could take to pursue a goal like "the greatest renown" was to exhibit their goal for others' consideration.

During roughly the same time period (1942-1950), UH student writing in *The Harvest* came to be presented as support for an argument for cultural and artistic freedom in the face of oppression. The 1942 issue's introduction consisted of uncharacteristically abstract and grandiose language to defend imaginative writing against the specters of censorship and despair. This introduction defends "understanding of the emotional, intellectual and spiritual aspects of life," which requires "the expression of one's self and … the interpretation of other selves," against the threat of "conflict, chaos, and destruction" (Hicks et al.). By 1943, references to World War II become more direct: "In this period of total war, we are told on every hand that all activities which occupy our time and efforts must be justified in terms of their contribution to the war effort" ("Staff," *The Harvest* 8). In contrast to book burning and the suppression of "intellectual liberty," the editors "offer 'THE HARVEST of 1943' as [their] contribution to total victory" (ibid). By 1944, several of the student contributions to *The Harvest* comment directly on the war while other contributions attempt "to escape from the war through humor" ("Preface," *The Harvest* 9). That year's issue was used to "throw a few rays of light upon the Human Miracle in its moment of trial" (ibid). The 1945 *Harvest* acknowledges both the crumbling of Fascism and the prominence of "escape literature" in its pages ("Preface," *The Harvest* 10). That year's student writings are presented as promoters of "the human mind and soul," in contrast to the goals of military aggression (ibid). By 1947, *The Harvest* featured writing from many World War II veterans, the issue's editors feeling "justified in publishing such material since over two-thirds of [the UH] study body are veterans, and many of them wish to write about their experiences while they are still fresh" ("Preface," *The Harvest* 12). Cumulatively, these references promote *The*

Harvest as a symbol of free expression despite the many filters through which student submissions passed before receiving public backing of faculty and administrators. If the 1940s saw *The Harvest* used as support for institutional value, it also saw *The Harvest* used to support a pro-democracy statement, yet another enhancement of the *Harvest*-UH image.

STUDENT WRITING, INSTITUTIONAL PUBLICITY

In a study of one Wisconsin normal college's student essays written in 1898 to commemorate state history, Kathryn Fitzgerald explains that writing assignments rooted in epideictic exigencies can lead to uncritical accounts of local history (123-24) and erase depictions of diverse people (131-32). She reminds us that normalizing influences of writing assignments that directly or indirectly encourage praise must always be scrutinized. Bearing in mind these and other risks of using student writing to demonstrate state (or institutional) value, I would add that we lose a powerful source of analysis if, from suspicion of epideixis, we neglect to study—and ask our students today to consider—uses to which student writing is put.

The examples that I review above come from student writing that was originally in or for undergraduate writing classes, yet for all of its ties to the classroom, the writing was also held up to impress extracurricular audiences. That action itself and the play of discursive emphasis that it involved become visible as strategic moves with multiple outcomes (to enhance students' reputations, to support institutional leaders' existing perceptions, to broaden understandings about what an institution does) once we view them via sophistic epideictic practices that scholars like Poulakos and McComiskey have analyzed anew in light of contemporary rhetorical concerns. At OU, faculty and administrators who wished to preserve a certain perspective of local historical events and portray a respectable scholarly image of first-year students could use students' three-volume institutional history to do so. At UH, faculty and administrators who wanted to build a case for diverse local talent at their institution could present students' writing to illustrate this. Obviously, students at OU and UH wrote more than the work that appeared in these publications, but the fact that details from these as opposed to other texts remain to contribute to institutional memory sends a message. Presented as they were, these student writing collections suggest that although their host university may have sought to improve the intellectual skills of students, another goal of the university was to maintain or enhance its institutional reputation. Student writing taken, it would appear, from the institution's writing classes proved a useful tool with which campus leaders could create displays of student value—of students who wrote like scholars or students whose varied life experiences fueled uncommonly gripping writing. By examining interactions between student writing and outwardly looking faculty and administrators, I create a space for classifying student writing as institutional public relations work, a twentieth-century parallel to early sophists' efforts to theatricalize, through careful selection and showing, the seemingly non-theatrical.

A constraint of this line of analysis is that I cannot identify who *actually* read OU's *Ohio University in the 1920s: A Social History* and *Ohio University in the Twentieth Century: A Fifty-Year History* and UH's *The Harvest*. But I contend that we nonetheless gain insight by gathering signs of these works' *intended* audiences, what Lisa Ede and Andrea Lunsford call the "audience invoked" (156)— or in the case of my analysis, the reader or readers imagined by faculty and administrator editors who influenced the student writing. While we cannot know every person whom faculty and administrators at OU and UH hoped to reach through the student writing that they sponsored, contributions from faculty and administrators reveal *kinds* of readers who were sought: readers who had familiarity with scholarly writing and readers who knew about the conditions of student writing at multiple universities. Whatever their exact constitution, the audiences envisioned by faculty and administrators matter, revealing clues about the motivations and strategies of institutional literacy sponsors in shaping student writing. Moreover, the fact that students at pre-1950s OU and UH may not have had the same audience awareness as their instructors and administrators deserves attention. Even if, as historians or instructors, we detect signs of an intended audience of people with knowledge of many colleges and universities, the students whom we study or teach may make sense of their writing, as well as their writing's influences and outcomes, through a far narrower frame of reference. Future studies focused on the relationship between student writing and institutional public relations statements might track signs of audience awareness both from students and from non-student literacy sponsors. From a sophistic epideictic tradition, I propose asking oneself (and in teaching situations, one's students), who is and who is not seeing, as well as who is and who is not supposed to see, any given display of institutional worth? Inquiry along these lines can productively complicate the notion that spectacles are created for a singular audience and produce a singular effect.

A more basic question that instructors who take up this analytical thread for present-day pedagogical purposes might ask is, in what ways do our students' papers lend themselves to showpieces that others can use to represent institutional success or excellence? Once we consider how student writing is presented (with whose endorsements and interpretations?) and distributed (to what actual or intended audiences? to what audiences that students know about?), we can begin to understand what the relationship between student writing and institutional public relations means for our students and institutions as the student writing circulates in a glocal environment. For students, it becomes one thing to write, another thing to be assisted and promoted, and yet another thing to reach audiences selected by others. Each of these activities reshapes the writing's spatial and rhetorical work.

CHAPTER FIVE
RETHINKING LINKS BETWEEN HISTORIES OF COMPOSITION

As Chapters Two through Four have shown, interactional patterns between historical college student writing and other people and ideas allow us to compare sites as different as a university in the borderland between the Midwest and Appalachia and a university in a major south-central city. The former, OU, witnessed years of westward migration in the nineteenth century, and the latter, UH, founded in the early twentieth century, witnessed an economic and demographic boom thereafter. Beyond already established similarities between how, at these universities, pre-1950s student writing expanded institutional nomoi, acted kairotically in reference to state or city concerns, and supported epideictic discourse, similarities arise if we dwell more fully on historiography than history. Given the sophistic tradition of framing and reframing knowledge based on language and convention, of finding a reality *through* discourse, as Antiphon illustrated in his *Tetralogies* (Tindale 100), we can consider what we gain if we reconceptualize universities themselves—for many of us, the primary site of our everyday work. More precisely, we can reframe who and what we mean when we refer to *college composition, composition instructors*, and *composition students*. The decades before the 1950s lend themselves well to this work because before composition grew into Composition, instructors who taught writing (or rhetoric) readily identified, or were identified, in several ways—as writing teachers as well as members of other professions and emerging disciplines, and as people who worked in classrooms, at community events, and at state or national meetings. At the same time, students wrote pieces for their writing classes but also identified with numerous on- and off-campus groups; even the category *English major* could take more capacious meanings than it holds today.

My goal in this chapter is not to tinker with terms and categories for the sake of tinkering, but, in the spirit of Christopher W. Tindale's reading of *Dissoi Logoi*, to consider other terms (i.e., other conceptions of composition instructors and students) in order to identify the terms' merits (Tindale 104). Recent Rhetoric and Composition research has already begun the important work of unsettling popular notions of writing instructors and students, categories that appear increasingly fluid as times goes on. For example, in "The Politics of Place: Student Travelers and Pedagogical Maps," Julie Drew examines the benefits of framing modern-day composition students as travelers traveling. As she puts it,

Chapter Five

> Students pass through, and only pause briefly within, classrooms; they dwell within and visit various other locations, locations whose politics and discourse conventions both construct and identify them. By reimagining students as travelers we may construct a politics of place that is more likely to include students in the academic work of composition, and less likely to continue to identify and manage students as discursive novices. (60)

This perspective frames composition students within and, more importantly, outside of classrooms. Thus, Drew discusses the potential of having students compare academically sanctioned discourses to "discourses in which students may feel both more familiar and privileged" (64), discourses common to locations other than the college writing classroom and where students may identify as experts or insiders instead of *students*.

In her conclusion, Drew acknowledges that instructors, too, may be framed as travelers, but she laments "[instructors'] own reluctance to see ourselves as performing our work, in a sense, on the road, in seeing ourselves as occupants of a place where students briefly pause—a roadside stand, perhaps—in their lifelong relationships with multiple discourses" (66). Whether instructors admit it, we, like other literacy sponsors, travel as we interact with people and places beyond students and writing classes. Additionally, as Jonathon Mauk argues, building on Edward Soja's *Thirdspace*, discourses and tangible, material factors intersect, so our notions of place must include both discourses and people, that is, bodies encountering new conditions that are felt and interpreted and then used to create new discourse-based understandings (Mauk 379). I think of the example of a college composition instructor who interacts with civic organizations that raise money for public libraries and neighborhood literacy groups—physical interactions with other people and in venues where the civic organizations meet. Before, during, and after these interactions, the college instructor may propose writing courses at her university, construct writing assignments, and advise her college students about mentoring and internships that centralize skills in writing and reading. That is, the instructor may create discourses capable of reflecting her newfound, and perhaps unacknowledged, associations. In such a case, material and discursive factors interact with the potential to influence each other.

In general, though, Mauk wants people to locate themselves less in terms of "the indicative (*what is*)" and more in terms of "the subjunctive (*what could be*)" (379), an orientation that could prompt composition students to explore *potential* meanings and uses of places as the students and others move—or travel. The concept of potentiality, which Drew, Mauk, and other Rhetoric and Composition scholars begin to unpack, informs this chapter's reframing of *composition*, *instructors*, and *students* based on the cases of pre-1950s OU and UH. But before turning to those historical details, we would do well to note a First Sophistic parallel to a contemporary understanding of potentiality, a parallel that clarifies what it can mean to apply the subjunctive (what could be) to composition historiography. Here I refer to dynaton, whose Greek root *dyn* is usually translated as *possible*. Near the beginning of *Gorgias*, Plato's Socrates uses dynaton when he asks the sophist Gorgias, "So then should we assert that you are *able* to make others rhetors too?" to which Gorgias concurs readily (449b, emphasis added). A more dramatic use of dynaton appears in *Theaetetus*, scholar Noburu Notomi informs us, when a "philosopher explains that to escape from earth to heaven … is to become as like a god as possible (*homoiōsis theōi kata to dynaton*, 176b1-3)" (Notomi 287). In these cases, dyanton focuses attention on the characteristic of ability and gestures to yet-to-be-revealed ideas or actions. Later, in Aristotle's *Metaphysics*, dynaton appeared in binary opposition to what Aristotle called *energeia*, or actuality (50b6), and this binary has informed subsequent understandings of dynaton.

Today, though we lack examples of ancient sophists introducing as opposed to consenting to the word *dynaton* in conversation, we do have examples of early sophists reasoning in ways that imply dynaton, as John Poulakos explains ("Toward a Sophistic Definition" 44-45). Most famously, Gorgias, in *The Encomium of Helen*, moves from repeating established facts about Spartan queen Helen's seduction by Prince Paris to speculating about multiple plausible interpretations of Helen's actions: "To tell the knowing what they know shows it is right but brings no delight" (5). A similar move marks Gorgias' defense of the proposal that speech itself, not simply Prince Paris, deserves blame in Helen's seduction. "What cause … prevents the conclusion that Helen … against her will, might have come under the influence of speech, just as if ravished by the force of the might?" he asks (12). And there begins a broader treatment, involving stimulating analogies, of the potential effects of speech. These moments, which Poulakos has already discussed in terms of the possible, join others of early sophists creating discursive spaces in which to consider novel or unusual factors ("Toward a Sophistic" 44) and thereby reframe the discussion at hand. In a later article, Poulakos observes that whereas the traditional orator in classical antiquity worked from established knowledge and "confine[d] [listeners] within those boundaries," the orator who was guided by dynaton acknowledged the impossibility of reaching all ideals yet nonetheless stressed the "'there', the 'then' and the 'can be'" ("The Logic" 21). The latter type of orator focused on moving audiences past constraints imposed by existing conventions, a focus demanding that the orator first understood and then thought imaginatively about those conventions. In

Poulakos' words, "If the orator's display succeeds in firing the imagination of his listeners, and if their hopes triumph over their experiences, the possibilities before them are well on their way to actualization" ("The Logic" 22).

For composition historiography, inspiring audiences to imagine a reachable but not yet flourishing "can be" might begin with the question, through what (if any) interpretive decisions are composition historians "firing the imagination" of readers and giving readers hope about new kinds of histories worth exploring? Patricia Donahue, in the final chapter of *Local Histories: Reading the Archives of Composition*, discusses the difficulty of breaking from Albert R. Kitzhaber's Harvard-based narrative of composition history. Nevertheless, instead of continuing to follow Kitzhaber's methodological choices, she proposes "an expanded analytical framework" that embraces "many possible sites of pedagogical innovation" (Donahue 223). If one still wishes to study the history of composition at Harvard, then one may at least study under-analyzed influences at that site, including influences from administrators and non-composition faculty members (Donahue 229-30). Another of her suggestions is to study the "migration" of early Harvard Professor Adams Sherman Hill's book *Principles of Rhetoric and Their Application* across institutional sites (231), an analytical approach that Drew and Mauk would frame as discourse (Hill's book) traveling across, and interacting with, physical sites (college campuses). Also, Donahue discusses the "opening up of new possibilities" from treating composition as a cultural practice grounded in teaching (235). Coursing through her many suggestions is the allure of untried possibilities in how scholars create composition histories.

Of course, composition historians have begun to consider voices not previously treated as valid contributors to the practice or teaching of writing (Ramsey et al.; Kirsch and Rohan, *Beyond*), and certainly feminist scholars (e.g., Mastrangelo; Bordelon; Enoch, *Refiguring*; Glenn and Enoch) have been at the forefront of this development. But even so, I think that our ways of thinking about historical information at and across institutional sites remain tied to conventional understandings of higher education institutions themselves. Commonly (we might say conventionally), scholars who study composition's past at more than one postsecondary institution focus on one natural or political region: three institutions in central-northern Illinois for Thomas M. Masters, three institutions in east and north Texas for David Gold. Or scholars who take up the study of composition history at multiple sites focus on institutions of the same kind: two Ivy League institutions for Kelly Ritter (*Before*), colleges for working-class students for Susan Kates. While parameters placed around familiar regions or around institutional types can focus a scholar's research and broaden readers' understanding of where and how composition has developed, other ways of focusing are possible.

In the remainder of this chapter, I heed the idea of dynaton by departing from comparisons preferred by most composition historians and instead opening up a lesser-known narrative path (see Jarratt, *Rereading* 28). My approach, unconstrained by disciplinary lines (Jarratt, *Rereading* 12) and commonsensical institutional similarities, tracks movements across physical and social places of people who administered, taught, or studied composition at pre-1950s OU and UH. The names of the people whom I consider appear across available historical records from or about each of these universities, and their movements covered places within and beyond any one institutional site. In the case of OU, I examine the movements of William Henry Scott, OU president from 1872 to 1883 and a key figure in expanding his university's financial base. I look at changes that Scott and his successors enabled at OU in the decades after his presidency, focusing on the fact that during this time composition grew in multiple directions simultaneously to serve the interests of faculty members from different OU departments and colleges. Then, in the case of UH, which lacks historical records of the same kind kept at OU, I focus on four people whose interactions brought composition into contact with yet other people and ideas. These four people were L. Standlee Mitchell, a professor, director, and actor who brought together rhetoric and drama; Harvey W. Harris, an instructor of speech and English who brought together oral and written rhetoric as well as classroom learning and extracurricular activities; Mary Treadway, a student at Houston Junior College who, as a recipient of a scholarship from a Houston-area women's club, brought together college writing and civic sponsorship; and Professor Ruth Pennybacker, whose teaching, education, and family connections brought together local and national movements. More than extracting composition insights from biographical sketches, a convention in both local and national histories (Kitzhaber 59; Connors 183; Varnum 38, 134; Kates 28; Gold 126; Masters 185), but also within the realm of the "can be" (Poulakos, "The Logic" 21), my focus encourages scholars to notice *glocal* travels of people and ideas, as well as kinds of influences that, regardless of region or institutional type, can structure the writing environments experienced by college students. Such travels would go undetected if I analyzed and compared OU and UH through the more expected factor of their surrounding region or institutional type. Too, as I show in this and the next chapter, recognizing composition's shifting shapes and influences creates new possibilities for historical information about composition to inform present-day practices.

COMPOSITION ON THE MOVE AT OU

At OU, shifting shapes of composition can be studied by first tracking the social and physical spaces entered by an influential university member, William

Chapter Five

Henry Scott, whose actions were reported across historical sources. From here, we can consider how Scott's work at and beyond OU connected to interactions that profoundly changed composition at his institution, putting the ownership of composition into the hands of numerous people as new departments, colleges, and course sequences emerged circa 1900. That is, at least two kinds of travels are conspicuous, the travels of Scott, president of OU from 1872 to 1883, and the travels of the *concept of composition* as it was taken up by institutional stakeholders in the decades after Scott's presidency.

WILLIAM HENRY SCOTT

Born in 1840, Scott graduated from OU in 1862 (he would become the first OU president to also be an alumnus of this institution). As numerous biographical sketches report, he then worked in the Athens public schools, became principal of OU's preparatory department, and served as a minister in Chillicothe, Ohio, and the state capital of Columbus before returning to OU in 1869 as a "Professor of Greek Language and Literature," one of two professors that year to have "literature" in his title (*Ohio University Bulletin, 1869-1870* 5). (In 1869, no faculty members had *composition, writing,* or *rhetoric* in their titles, though students took classes in rhetoric and literature and in composition in English and classical languages. Course titles included "English Grammar," "English Composition," "Rhetoric and English Literature" [18], and "Forensics and Original Declamations" [19].) In 1872, upon becoming acting president of OU and professor of intellectual and moral philosophy (*Ohio University Bulletin, 1872-1873* 5), Scott began traveling between Athens and Columbus, a trip of over seventy miles each way, for a targeted purpose: to lobby for increased financial support from the state legislature. From Chapter Two, we might recall Scott's 1873 student Margaret Boyd, who wrote in her diary on Friday, January 24, "Scott has been at Columbus seeing about the interest of the college," among similar observations that semester. Scott's absences from Athens and thus from the elocution class that Boyd and other students took in Spring 1873 proved noteworthy to Boyd, and very possibly for other students, for its ability to alter classroom protocol.

Scott's lobbying produced modest results in the form of additional annual income to the university and funds to repair campus buildings (T. Hoover 143-44, 147; Super 62; Taylor 909), yet more important than those results was the tradition of traveling and lobbying that he normalized at OU. Later presidents, especially presidents Super and Ellis, would pick up where Scott left off and secure significant new revenue sources, establishing the financial base necessary to grow the faculty and multiply the departments and colleges. Scott's 1883 successor, Charles William Super, wrote that as president, Scott was a "financial agent" and a "perpetual lobbyist, as the [state] legislature met every year and the lobbying could not all be done at Columbus" (66). Super added, "[Scott] was expected to be everywhere and was assumed to be responsible for everything that was what it should not" (66). The responsibility that Super references gains meaning when we realize that, in Super's words, "almost to the end of the nineteenth century the O.U. received no private donations" (74). In short, state funding operated as a lifeline to OU.

Without getting bogged down in the minutiae of legislative debates from the 1870s to the early 1900s, we should notice two changes approved by the State of Ohio that allocated significant amounts of money from selected taxes to OU and its sister institution, Miami University. First was the Sleeper Bill of 1896, which was viewed by historian Thomas Nathaniel Hoover as an outgrowth of President Super's efforts to secure financial appropriations from the state (T. Hoover 161). Second, becoming law in 1902 and vigorously supported by OU President Ellis (T. Hoover 180), was the Seese Bill, which made a "provision for a State Normal College in connection with [Ohio] University, and [gave] for its support an annual revenue of about $38,000" (Taylor 909). Throughout this time, Presidents Super and Ellis followed Scott's earlier example by devoting time and energy to persuading state legislators to support OU, even traveling to Columbus during critical periods (see T. Hoover 180). Years before their presidencies, Scott's "persistent efforts to secure an endowment" (T. Hoover 147) had included "begg[ing] the trustees" to convince legislators to heed their concerns (146) as well as attending state legislative sessions, even delivering the "prayer at the opening of the sessions" (147). With OU's state-supported growth came new possibilities for composition, ways that college student writing could be attached to various professors and to course sequences with burgeoning enrollments. Nowhere do the interdisciplinary developments of composition in the post-Scott years appear as tellingly as in OU catalogs. So here I follow changes in catalog references to college student writing, often but not necessarily designated by the term *composition*.

CATALOG-BASED COMPOSITION

Between 1900 and 1950, the province of composition appears to stretch and bend given its relationship to subjects such as literature, creative writing, business, grammar, rhetoric, and teacher training, as faculty members in the decades after Scott's reign harnessed composition to fit their newly supported specializations. OU's Commercial College, formed in the 1890s, took composition in one direction, while its State Normal College, the degree-granting successor to the 1886-founded Normal Department, took composition in another direction; furthermore, composition continued to be taught in the College of Liberal Arts. The liberal arts treatment of composition appears in the 1901-1902 Catalog's description of the Department of Rhetoric and English Literature:

> The aim of the English Department is two-fold, to train the power of expressing thought, and to cultivate an appreciation of literature. In the classes in Rhetoric the main stress is placed upon the actual work in composition done by the student. In the study of Literature the endeavor is to quicken the artistic and aesthetic sense. (26)

Shortly thereafter, the Catalog relates, "*When studying Literature, emphasis will also be placed upon the practice of composition, and in the classes in Rhetoric much attention will be given to the study of Literature*" (26). As this section illustrates, the Department of Rhetoric and English Literature of the College of Liberal Arts framed composition in terms of its service to rhetoric and literature. Students studied rhetoric by composing, and students studied literature through, or in addition to, "the practice of composition." Students taking courses from the English department's curriculum had to complete six prerequisites, the first and sixth of the courses called "Composition and Rhetoric" (no description given); the remaining prerequisites consisted of English and American literature. In the Department of Rhetoric and English Literature's regular courses was "College Writing," which "plac[ed] stress upon paragraph-writing" (27). After this, students took "Public Speaking and Argumentation," which provided "training in public speaking, special stress being placed upon argumentation" (27). Not a logic course, the description continues, Public Speaking and Argumentation focused on "the principles of argumentation as used in every-day life" and required students to participate at least once in a "public debate given in the University Auditorium" (27). Other courses in the College of Liberal Arts in 1901-1902 dwelt on canonized literary works.

By contrast, OU's Commercial College, offering two years of preparatory courses followed by two years of regular college courses, approached composition in terms of its uses in specific professional capacities, usually capacities that privileged writing technologies. In 1901-1902, the Commercial College had three faculty members (compared to two faculty members in the College of Liberal Arts' Department of Rhetoric an English Literature), one of them in Stenography and Typewriting and the other of them in Penmanship. Another difference from the College of Liberal Arts was that the Commercial College prescribed "Elementary Rhetoric," which involved five recitations per week and was taken in the first term of one's first year of study (58). In the third term of one's second year, the College prescribed "Advanced Rhetoric," also involving five recitations per week (58). In other words, the preparatory half of the Commercial College's course sequence began and ended with rhetoric classes, and each class was labeled so as to convey a progression: elementary to advanced. If a progression was intended in the College of Liberal Arts' courses on composition or rhetoric, then it escapes notice in course titles. Moreover, students in the Commercial College never strayed from an emphasis on writing, often writing via mastery of new technologies for producing text. Whereas students in the College of Liberal Arts prepared to write paragraphs and participate in oral debates, students in the Commercial College familiarized themselves with rhetorical principles before turning attention to the physical properties of writing in society. Commercial College students took both Freshman English (involving three recitations per week) and Penmanship during all three terms of their third year of coursework; then students took Stenography (with five recitations per week) and, across three consecutive terms, Typewriting (59). This sequence of courses situated writing in a world that extended beyond academic conventions.

Finally, and most tellingly, the rise of elaborate course sequences in education at OU, when the State Normal College was founded in 1902, gave composition and rhetoric another slant—pairing it with teacher training and exposing it to a greater number of students, especially female students. This was eleven years before Ohio's first independent state normal college was founded in Kent to the north and twelve years before its second independent state normal college was founded in Bowling Green to the northwest (see Ogren 227). Although since the early-mid 1800s Ohio had had private normal *schools* as well as nondegree teacher training programs within public universities, including Ohio University (Ogren 17), 1902 marks the first time when a state-sponsored, degree-granting college within a university in Ohio appeared and therefore the first time when such a configuration could shape public college students and their writing. OU's Summer School, for example, posted gains in both its overall student population and in its female student population in the years around 1902. The Summer School population was 38% female in 1899. By 1903, the Summer School population had grown to 62% female, and by 1906 it was 68% female (*Ohio University Bulletin, 1906-1907*). These changes extend Christine A. Ogren's finding, based on several institutions across the country, that women comprised the majority of state normal school populations from 1870 to 1910 (65). OU had had a Department of Pedagogy since the 1880s, but the pace of change in the university's overall student population, course offerings, and stance toward teacher education increased markedly in the wake of the Seese Bill-founded State Normal College. The 1901-1902 Catalog explained, "it is proposed to make [the new Normal College] somewhat broader and more distinctively professional than that of the present Pedagogical Course of the University" (77). The Normal College appeared to pursue this breadth and professionalism by offering students a two-year course sequence equivalent to high school or preparatory courses, completion of which earned students a diploma. A second option in the Normal College existed for short-term studies, and yet another option was "a more thorough professional course, covering a full four-year period and, while clearly differentiated from them, the equal, in scholarship and training power, of any of the existing college courses. This course will lead to the degree of *Bachelor of Pedagogy*" (77). One of the greatest changes between the old Department of Pedagogy and the new Normal College was that the latter claimed equality with the other colleges at OU. Additionally, catalog listings after 1902 suggest that the Normal College took composition as or more seriously than the College of Liberal Arts did.

To appreciate the new directions in which the Normal College took composition, we should first notice the relative stagnancy in the College of Liberal Arts' treatment of composition. In 1902-1903, as in previous years, the College of Liberal Arts included "Composition and Rhetoric" as the first and sixth courses in its preparatory course sequence. One change introduced at this time was that by 1902-1903 the Composition and Rhetoric course to be taken in one's sixth term bore the catalog description, "a study of Description, Narration, Exposition, and Argumentation" (*Ohio University Bulletin, 1902-1903* 30). Changes in the College of Liberal Arts' Rhetoric and English Literature Department included the fact that the department's fall-term course College Writing had become College Rhetoric and now focused on "paragraph-writing and editorials" (30) as opposed to paragraph writing alone. Also, by 1902-1903, this course included a parenthetical notation marking it "required for all degrees" (30), and the department made minor adjustments to its literature course sequence.

By contrast, the State Normal College of 1902-1903 did not frequently use the words *composition* and *rhetoric* in catalog descriptions; however, this college's perspective on teaching methods amounts to a surprisingly evolved, nuanced view of rhetorical practices. Here, clearly, attention to actions that fit specific purposes, audiences, and interests came to the fore. As the term *methods* was used in the Normal College's descriptions of its mission and courses, it constituted one's ability to see connections among ideas and academic areas:

> instruction must concern itself with the development of human life, show how it manifests itself in the various occupations demanded by its nature, and how its growth is determined by geographical conditions. Here should be pointed out how geographical surroundings determine the occupations of men, affect their habits, promote their desires, restrain their ambi-

tions, and establish their supremacy or bondage. (75)

Implicit in this account is the role of location and social status in influencing people's tastes and ideas. The account's focus on situational factors and use of inductive thinking continues when it discusses methods for teaching history:

> The teaching of history begins not with the book, but with the experiences of life. It should point out how law and order display themselves in the family, social, religious, and political life, and how they reflect various stages of thought and action. It should show how these institutions enhance the individuality of man, and how they are in turn reflected in and exemplified by him. (75)

Unlike descriptions of OU's College of Liberal Arts, these descriptions placed knowledge and everyday practices in history and in social configurations. And unlike many state normal schools' use of *methods* to mean the best way to teach a subject to a particular grade (Ogren 127), the meaning used by OU's State Normal College paired reading and writing with situated knowledge structures.

The Normal College of 1902-1903, like the College of Liberal Arts, offered courses in composition and rhetoric more heavily during students' earlier years of study. (Generally, students in the College of Liberal Arts took one class called "College Rhetoric" and no additional coursework in this area.) However, an important difference between the colleges was that the Normal College kept an eye on composition and rhetoric in students' mid-to-later years of coursework. The fullest attention that the Normal College gave to composition and rhetoric in its course offerings was in its course sequence for Elementary Education, entrance to which depended on graduation from a common school. But lest we conclude from this modest entrance requirement that the Elementary Education course sequence was entirely introductory, we should observe that students from more advanced course sequences could, with faculty approval, take courses in this sequence (137). In the courses for the Elementary Education sequence, we find

- Rhetoric and Composition taken in the spring term of one's first year, with five hours of work per week to be devoted to this subject
- Penmanship taken in the spring term of one's first year
- Rhetoric taken in the spring term of one's third year
- *Methods* in Reading and Composition taken in the fall term of one's fourth year, with three hours of work per week to be devoted to this subject
- College Rhetoric in the fall term of one's fifth year (132-33, emphasis added)

Chapter Five

In addition, sprinkled across the five years of courses were more methods courses in subjects such as history and mathematics, the relevance of which grows when we recall the rhetorically rich description of *methods* used by the Normal College.

By 1905, OU found itself with two separate and simultaneously operating Departments of English, a situation not unheard of at the time. In her study of composition history at Massachusetts' Wellesley College, Lisa Mastrangelo found as many as three departments of English functioning simultaneously in 1906-1907, one department focused on literature, a second focused on language, and a third focused on composition (96). But the dual English departments at OU give us a surprising case of an English department in an education college, more so than an English department in a liberal arts college, pushing composition to the center of its curriculum. The 1923 student yearbook *The Athena*, published soon after the Normal College had transformed to OU's College of Education, summarized this development as follows:

> English was given a department in the College of Education in 1905. Before that time English Composition and Literature had been given in the College of Arts, and courses in methods, in the College of Education.
>
> With the growth of the University and the College of Education, it became necessary to have a department of English in the College of Education. There are now 450 students in the English Composition courses of the department.
>
> This department has for its aims the development of expression, oral and written, and the acquiring of a love for good literature. It gives special attention to the methods of teaching English subjects. (*Athena* 72)

Here the development of the Normal College's English Department is linked to the "growth of the University and the College of Education," an increase in the number of students who hoped to benefit from formal training in teaching methods. Also, the writers refer to composition in conjunction with the department's total number of students, 450, and the writers acknowledge the department's aims (see Fig. 4).

In 1923, the College of Education-run English department was advertised as having four faculty members, just shy of the five faculty members in the English department of the College of Liberal Arts (*Athena*). Additionally, the student writers of the 1923 *Athena* offer little description of what actually transpired in the College of Liberal Arts' English Department, what priorities the department

Rethinking Links Between Histories of Composition

held dear, instead giving the names of the department's past faculty members and noting historical facts such as when OU faculty members first taught En-

Figure 4. English Department of the Ohio University College of Education, Athena, 1923. Courtesy of the University Archives, Mahn Center for Archives and Special Collections, Ohio University Libraries.

glish "as a subject" (in 1860) and when the faculty members first taught English Literature (in 1862) (51). Figure 5 illustrates such differences. Between the depictions of the two English departments in the 1923 *Athena*, it was the College of Education that articulated the *purpose* of its English department more fully.

Insofar as course descriptions speak, those of OU's State Normal College circa 1920 provide what by modern standards is a more compelling vision of composition than those of the College of Liberal Arts. For example, in 1919-1920, the College of Liberal Arts offered a two-course sequence of Freshman English, which had "two definite purposes: (a) The endeavor to increase the student's power of self-expression through emphasis upon practice in oral and written composition; (b) A systematic preliminary survey of English literature" (49)—that is, an emphasis on literature and on self-expression that interweaves composition, literature, and, implicitly, rhetoric in ways consonant with the 1901-1902 Catalog. Meanwhile, the 1919-1920 Normal College offered its own two-course sequence of first-year composition, "Freshman Composition, Teachers' Course," the first of which focused on "oral and written composition in narration and exposition" and the second of which focused on "oral and written work in description and argumentation" (133). The descriptions of Freshman Composition, Teachers' Course, show the Normal College tying composition to oral rhetoric much as the College of Liberal Arts did. But unlike the College of Liberal Arts of 1919-1920, the Normal College's English department specified modes of discourse that it taught, and this English department began to trouble the tendency to esteem imaginative literature (canonized fiction and poetry) above all else. Indicative of the latter is the fact that the Normal College's English department of 1919-1920 offered a course for juniors and seniors called "The English Essay of the Nineteenth Century," which focused on "the leading essayists and literary movements of the Victorian Age" (134). Allowing attention to nonfiction prose, this course had no equivalent in the College of Liberal Arts' Department of English Language and Learning. Although the College of Liberal Arts' English department did offer a course called "Advanced Composition," this course "deal[t] mainly with the Short Story" (51) and thus treated composition as fiction writing. Alone, each of these observations says little, but when compiled for comparison they allow us to ask whether the College of Liberal Arts was ceding composition, viewed as the production of nonfiction text, to the State Normal College.

The 1919-1920 course titles above persisted through the 1920s, and by 1925-1926 the College of Education offered an assortment of courses on the essay, including English Essay of the Victorian Period and English Essay of the Eighteenth Century, as well as a Literature and Advanced Composition course whose scope included essays and fictional forms and whose assignments spanned "creative and critical writing" (*Ohio University Bulletin, 1925-1926* 164). Also, College of Education students who took the course Teaching of Language in

Figure 5. English Department of the Ohio University College of Liberal Arts, Athena, 1923. Courtesy of the University Archives, Mahn Center for Archives and Special Collections, Ohio University Libraries.

the Junior High School focused on the topics of "composition as a social study, drills, freedom and accuracy in expression with study of models, spelling problems" (164). Mechanical though this last class may have become, it also gave attention to "freedom" in composing. No such course was listed under the English department of the College of Liberal Arts, whose students had to take College of Education courses as electives if the students wished to step outside of studies of imaginative prose and poetry. Other clues from 1925-1926 suggesting that the College of Education viewed the work of composition differently from its Liberal Arts counterpart include the College of Education's stipulation that "a student must have an average of 'C' or above, or a 'C' or above in his last course in English composition before he may do student teaching in any school" (123). Moreover, those students who wished to obtain a Bachelor of Science degree in education had to take two "Freshman Composition" courses and two literature courses, and those students who sought to teach English in high schools had to meet additional English requirements. Finally, in 1925-1926, the College of Education offered "Sub-Freshman Composition," the only developmental writing course in that year's catalog, described as "a course planned for those whose preparation has been insufficient to meet the demands of [first-year composition, here the version of first-year composition offered by the College of Education]. No credit" (163). The fact that this college alone offered developmental writing points to how it connected its mission to composition: College of Education faculty members treated their intellectual purview as entailing both the *preparation* of college students *for* college-level writing and the *instruction* of college students *in* college-level writing. By 1927, catalogs show that the College of Liberal Arts began offering a developmental writing course that was described in nearly identical terms as the one offered by the College of Education a year earlier, perhaps an attempt from the College of Liberal Arts to keep up.

Drawing cause-effect connections between President Scott's 1870s-1880s lobbying of state legislators and OU's early 1900s treatment of composition in its colleges and departments is unachievable right now. But the analysis unfolding here, which privileges signs of influence instead of a single and presumably knowable cause and effect (Jarratt, *Rereading* 17), illustrates how a historical narrative anchored by dyanton can begin to develop. Such a narrative recalls Gorgias' work to complicate causal chains (Jarratt, *Rereading* 17), and it extends the possibility-generating project to the history of composition. From this OU narrative emerges a picture of college composition comprised of moving people and ideas, with a lobbying tradition normalized by Scott serving as at least one factor in enabling his successors to oversee rapid and significant growth in students, colleges, departments, and course options. In turn, these factors appear to have allowed composition to take many forms and meet many academic and professional needs. Seeing this string of associations reminds us that even though many early normal schools or normal programs embraced change, as David Gold has shown (119), such an embrace was not merely or necessarily a product of a disciplinary outlook. At OU, the rise in state funding and the popularity of teacher training programs allowed faculty members and administrators to do numerous things with composition—to try out multiple conceptions of composition and multiple placements of composition in newly created curriculums. Also, contrary to John C. Brereton's claim that composition after 1900 suffered "real damage" from its association with pedagogy (22; see also Masters 50), the case of OU allows us to see composition on the upswing, propelled by the direction of OU's 1880s-1920s financial and student growth that favored the State Normal College.

COMPOSITION BEYOND COURSEWORK AT UH

Unlike at OU, many of UH's earliest catalogs lack details, and course information takes the form of abbreviations and numbers. So I turn to travels of people whose names appear repeatedly across historical sources, such as the student newspaper *The Cougar* and the student yearbook *The Houstonian*, and whose names appear in association with college student writing. I see this shift in foci and source types as a way to apply the concept of dynaton to this research site: the shift lets me propose insights and idea connections that, based on available sources here, are neither known (what existing composition scholarship has established without question) nor merely ideal (what cannot under any circumstances be known). Revealing influences from other disciplines, departments, professions, and sections of the city and country, this evidence prompts us to consider how networks of composition scholars and instructors (e.g., Mastrangelo 61) can be enriched by extra-disciplinary contact. The figures singled out below show not only interactions between college students and different kinds of non-UH affiliates, but also opportunities for composition at UH to achieve new ends.

L. STANDLEE MITCHELL

Tracking 1930s HJC and UH faculty member L. Standlee Mitchell, who taught first-year composition as well as drama, means noticing influences from professional and community theater on HJC and UH students. It means, in effect, connecting the worlds of acting, directing, and local theater production to composition classes. Officially, Mitchell is remembered for chairing the UH Department of Drama from 1932 to 1950 and for serving as Dean of Men in the late 1940s. Education papers that he left behind, including papers for teaching purposes and papers showing his own learning as a student, support the claim that he took writing seriously, and this claim stands even if we disregard his writing about theater. Among his education papers is a collection of short biographies and poems by Texans about Texas, for example, "Texas," by Mary Saunders, which describes the beauty of the state's natural landscapes. Also, Mitchell kept a list titled "Texas Poets of Past and Present" and a paper, "The Personal Relations of Whitman and Emerson," which Mitchell himself wrote as a student (Mitchell). The latter earned him a grade of B, and his instructor commented that overall the paper was "well ordered, well written" (Mitchell).

As a teacher of first-year composition, or simply "English" as it was sometimes called in *The Cougar*, Mitchell was remembered for his interpersonal flair. In October 1934, one *Cougar* article summarized his teaching as follows: "If you think English is dull, register in Mr. Mitchell's class. After listening to him for a while you will go back for more English as well as atmosphere" ("Rambling"). After then relating an off-color joke that Mitchell made in class one day (an unacceptable joke by today's standards because it singled-out an African American student for linguistic ridicule), the article concludes, "No dull moments in Mr. Mitchell's room" (ibid). If this student account accurately conveys some of the most striking features of Mitchell's teaching style, then Rhetoric and Composition scholars today may feel tempted to view Mitchell's teaching as an example of the "entertainer's stance," Wayne C. Booth's 1963 category describing "the willingness to sacrifice substance to personality and charm" (144). However, Booth's bifurcation of style and substance fails to do justice to Mitchell's influence on the rhetorical education of students once we heed Mitchell's interactions beyond the classroom.

Bearing in mind that composition in the 1930s was not necessarily controlled by people with specialized training in rhetoric, and definitely not training in writing processes, rhetorical grammar, and so on, we should notice instructors' many ways of reaching students and of connecting students to the discursive and material worlds that the instructors inhabited. In Mitchell's case, there was his work as director of UH's John R. Bender Dramatic Club, which the 1934 *Houstonian* called "instrumental in giving the University some very fine entertainment in the way of plays." In February 1934, *The Cougar* described a speech given by Mitchell to thank members of one of his recent plays and, suggesting Mitchell's dedication to this line of work, related his announcement of "the intention of the club to start work immediately on another drama" ("Dramatic Club"). But it was his talent as an actor that temporarily drew him away from UH and into public entertainment A March 1934 article in *The Cougar*, "Mitchell Acclaimed as Matinee Idol," reported: "Mr. L. Standlee Mitchell, popular Junior College professor of Freshman English and dramatics, has accepted the leading role in Catamount Cinema Col's current colossal epic, 'Desert Nights,' Dean N. K. Dupre announced today. [Mitchell] will emote opposite that seductive siren, Gertie Gabbo" ("Mitchell Acclaimed"). The article continued,

> Mr. Mitchell was "discovered" by … an agent from the Catamount Studios who, while attending Junior College assembly, heard him recite that flowers poem, "Ten Nights in a Bathroom." His inimitable rendition so impressed [the agent] that [Mitchell] immediately signed for the leading role in his company's ned [sic] desert opus. Mr. Mitchell will take the part of a young Abrain shiek [sic] who captures a beautiful English woman and holds her for ransom. But when her husband, the gouty old Duke arrives with the money, a romance has blossomed between the desert chieftain and his lovely captive. The heroine decides to renounce her peerage and remain to find happiness in the arms of her true love. (ibid)

The article ends by reporting that production on the drama would wait until Mitchell finished the current school term and that UH would miss him. Yet if Mitchell left, he returned by October of that year because by then he reappeared in articles in *The Cougar*.

At issue given my interest in Mitchell's movements is that UH students, here students who wrote for their school newspaper, noticed some of the associations to which Mitchell's work led him. Much as some of the students lauded Mitchell's teaching for its entertainment value and invited more students to experience his classes first hand, the students commended Mitchell's activity in drama for attracting, through a studio agent, a broader public. The fact that Mitchell later returned to UH further supports the possibility that his trans-site and transdisciplinary movements bore on student writing at UH.

Harvey W. Harris

Although identified first and foremost as a speech instructor and debate coach, Harvey W. Harris, or "Mr. Harris" as he was referenced in student publications, was the only faculty member listed in the 1928 *Cougar* as instructor of HJC's two Composition and Rhetoric courses, English 113 and 123, and he was only instructor listed as teaching English 213, a survey of English literature ("Period to Be Hour"). English 113 was described as "A study of the principles of good writing, analysis and discussion of the representative English and American essays; special emphasis on Exposition and Argumentation; one thousand pages of outside reading; weekly themes." Its more advanced partner, English 123, was described as "A continuation of English 113; emphasis on Description and Narration; study of representative short stories; weekly themes; collateral reading" (ibid). So in 1928, the person charged with leading HJC students through weekly theme writing, exemplary literature, and expository and argumentative writing followed by descriptive and narrative writing was a faculty member whose commitments were split between writing and reading on the one hand and speech, mainly extracurricular speech, on the other hand.

Harris' speech commitments were multiple and significant. From Chapter Two, we might recall the comments in the 1934 *Cougar* about demand for Harris' speech classes: "Due to an overcrowded condition in Public Speaking I, the class has been divided into three sections with a chairman over each section. Mr. Harris, instructor, tries to be present in all three classes simultaneously, and comes nearer to accomplishing that feat than one might think" ("Rambling"). That same year, Harris sponsored a group called the Speakers' Club, which "held regular meetings throughout the school year," meetings "devoted to discussions of every day [sic] problems for the purpose of speech improvement. In addition to training, the club also sponsored a number of social events during the 1933-'34 term" (*Houstonian*). Additionally, the 1934 UH yearbook lists Harris as coach of UH's Oratorical Association, containing thirteen students, four of them women. The organization was

> composed of all the people interested in public speaking. This organization has been instrumental in making the school known in the field of debate. The school has participated in eight debates, having lost only two.
>
> During the year elimination contests were held on each question, thus giving each member an opportunity to represent the College in intercollegiate debates. (ibid)

The description concludes, "This organization combines the features of each variety of debating society to produce something both unusual and helpful to the students of the College" (ibid). Thus, acting as a speech coach, writing instructor, and literature instructor, as well as promoter of UH's student activities on and off campus, Harris shows another way that composition could interact with other sectors of academe and student life before the rise of an academic field called Rhetoric and Composition.

If the roles above failed to fill Harris' time, he had the added duty in 1928 of chairing HJC's Social Committee (Shepperd). Between this responsibility and the social side of his Speakers' Club involvement, he appears to have co-planned student activities, a job that would now belong to a staff member with graduate training in higher education and student affairs. And based on the following observation from the student newspaper, Harris' roles were appreciated: "An affable and a valuable organizer, a promoter and a dependable coworker is found in Prof. Harris, who also knows his stuff on salesmanship." Then the writer adds a specific point of praise: "When the committees on dance programs and ticket sales follow [Harris'] advice, increased attendance is noted at every fair" ("Introducing—Our Faculty").

One consequence of Harris' work at HJC and UH was that his students' education was informed by experiences gained off campus, even beyond Houston, such as when students debated members of other colleges and universities. One such occurrence received favorable coverage in a 1928 *Cougar* article, "U.T. [University of Texas] Debators Lose to H.J.C.," which related, "H. W. Harris, instructor in public speaking, former coach of the varsity coach [sic] of the Houston Junior College debating team at Texas, and now team [sic], revealed plans for bringing the Southwest Texas State Teachers college debaters to Houston within the next few weeks" ("U.T."). But off-campus influences also affected HJC students indirectly, through Harris' experiences and reputation and thus his ability to draw outsiders to HJC. One 1929 issue of *The Cougar* described Harris as follows: "head of Public Speaking, received his M. A. degree from the University of Texas. Mr. Harris is widely known as a public speaker and lecturer" (*The Cougar*, 1929). In light of Harris' responsibilities and accomplishments, we may revisit the simple descriptions for English 113 and English 123, both called Composition and Rhetoric, and propose the possibility—alongside multi-site and multi-disciplinary possibilities generated by tracking L. Standlee Mitchell—that Harris bridged the courses with developments from public speaking. An analysis of the course lists alone, without tracking Harris' many activities, fails to open up this HJC/UH narrative to the array of factors that likely colored how students viewed the work and place of writing.

Mary Treadway

If the physical, professional, and disciplinary travels of Harris and Mitchell show directions in which composition headed under the influence of charismatic and devoted instructors, 1930s student Mary Treadway shows how student writing could connect to drama at HJC and UH as well as how city literacy clubs could support student writing. In 1934, Treadway served as a member of Mitchell's Dramatic Club and a member of the Student Council (*Houstonian*). In addition to attending meetings of these clubs, she delivered a congratulatory address after one of the Dramatic Club's plays ("Dramatic Club"). In moments like this, we begin to see Treadway's contributions to the clubs as part of

115

Chapter Five

a rhetorical education broadly conceived, an education involving skillful writing and speaking for occasions beyond the writing classroom. Furthermore, her involvement in these student activities acquires wider significance once we notice that Treadway received an academic scholarship from the Houston Delphian Assembly, a local chapter of a national women's organization ("Organizational Information"), and that the Houston Delphian Assembly took a special interest in female students who demonstrated creative or artistic promise. At its 1933-34 meetings, assembly members discussed Treadway's talents in the area of music, particularly voice. By a March 1934 meeting, the members reported, "Mary Treadway ha[s] been elected president of her class in Junior College" (ibid). In March 1935, the assembly members announced that Treadway had "given up her scholarship" and that the scholarship would now transfer to another female student (ibid). In subsequent years, the assembly members would go on to fund not one student at a time, but up to twenty students during any given year.

Treadway's sponsorship by the Houston Delphian Assembly is a case of a civic organization with national ties supporting a UH student and monitoring the student's movement into leadership positions. Although the assembly neglected to single out English majors for scholarships, it supported college-facilitated writing or rhetoric in other ways. Created to develop a creative writing guild with a dramatic emphasis, the assembly looked for students who showed potential in these areas, according to a 1935 statement by the assembly's president. In practical terms, the assembly supported, even worked at, UH performing arts events such as operas (Williamson); funded scholarships; and gave money to the Departments of Biology, Speech Pathology-Audiology, and Arts, as well as to the UH library ("Houston Delphian"). Singling out and supporting sectors of HJC and UH such as the library and the arts, the assembly sponsored what today we might call a literacy education or, if recognizing the interplay of the political and the poetic, a rhetorical education. After all, as part of her student activities, Treadway created texts (e.g., speeches) in order to achieve a particular goal. Too, the fact that students at HJC and UH were required to complete first-year composition suggests that even students who were enrolled in this course may have received financial support and regular check-ins from the Houston Delphian Assembly.

Students' contact with this local chapter of a national women's group, a chapter that encouraged students' movement through classes and student organizations, alerts us to local-*but-not-just*-local interests that bore on some students as they wrote, spoke, and otherwise interacted with texts at HJC and UH. Given the Houston Delphian Assembly's literacy sponsorship, it begins to seem less surprising or inevitable that other historical records at UH show creative writing to have been alive and well in and beyond classes called composition, from the 1930s on. At least part of the rising visibility of creative writing, which other colleges and universities witnessed during the early-mid 1900s (Ritter, *To Know*; Myers), might be attributed to interests taken by civic organizations.

RUTH PENNYBACKER

Finally, composition at UH can be seen anew if we track an English department faculty member who traveled locally and nationally, someone who brought influences from many other people and places when she joined the UH faculty in 1935. I refer to Ruth Pennybacker, a Texas-raised Vassar graduate who taught first-year composition and creative writing and who, as Chapter Four discussed, sponsored UH's first literary magazine, *The Harvest*. Of all the faculty members whose names circulate around issues of student writing in the UH archives, Ruth's (I use her first name to distinguish her from her mother, Anna Pennybacker) is arguably the most prominent. Even now, I hear tell of early UH alumni who sang Ruth Pennybacker's praises for, among other actions, entering students in national writing contests and otherwise valuing students' writing.

One of the interactions that appears repeatedly in accounts of Ruth's life is the interaction between Ruth and her mother, Anna Pennybacker (often referred to as "Mrs. Percy V. Pennybacker" in newspaper articles), a figure known across Texas and eventually across the nation. A graduate of Texas' second-oldest normal school, Sam Houston Normal Institute (Ogren 232), now Sam Houston State University located seventy miles north of Houston, Anna became a teacher in a rural Texas school where her husband served as principal. Early biographer Helen Knox claims that Anna quickly gained respect through her oratorical skills, for example, by telling ghost stories to her students on the first day of class or, when dealing with adults, by supporting her points with stories about famous figures such as Napoleon (Knox). She gained the respect of other Texas citizens by speaking at the Texas State Teachers' Association about the power of education to teach patriotism and "true citizenship" (qtd. in Knox 62) and by writing a textbook, *A New History of Texas for Schools*, which was soon adopted by schools across the state and praised for evoking "Texas spirit" (Knox 86). But most important for my purposes is the fact that from 1912 to 1916 Anna served as president of the National Federation of Women's Clubs, an association that sponsored regular meetings of women who sought self- and civic improvement, from bodily and home cleanliness to fundraising for neighborhood libraries, to events that brought in out-of-town speakers to discuss topics of wide public concern. Given her status as a women's club president, a letter from Anna Pennybacker could garner local or national attention, as evidenced in her monthly letters published in the *Ladies' Home Journal* and in her letters to certain Houston-area women's clubs ("Twenty-Six"). In recent scholarly work, too, Anna

Pennybacker appears when, for instance, Anne Ruggles Gere introduces the first chapter of her book-length history of women's clubs by quoting from one of Anna Pennybacker's articles published in the 1918 *General Federation of Women's Clubs Magazine* (Gere 19-20).

During certain points in her own lifetime, Anna's presence eclipsed that of her daughter in published accounts of their civic work. Newspaper articles across the country, from small-town Texas papers to the *New York Times*, announced talks that the two gave together and often introduced Ruth in terms of her mother—Ruth as the daughter of the "past president of the General Federation of Women's Clubs," as one 1931 *Pittsburgh Press* article put it ("Southwestern"). Also in the 1930s, Ruth entered the distinguished society of First Lady Eleanor Roosevelt, likely owing to Anna's associations with the Roosevelts (see "Mrs. Pennybacker, Club Leader"; "Mrs. Pennybacker Dies"). For example, in 1931 the *New York Times* reported that Ruth, a "lecturer on literary topics and personalities," was to be a special guest at a luncheon given by Eleanor Roosevelt ("Mrs. Roosevelt"). Without negating daughter Ruth's ability to write and network, I want to point out that Ruth joined the UH faculty while her nationally known mother was still alive and, partly due to that fact, was a well-connected hire. One late-twentieth-century UH historian wrote that Ruth "knew many of the [Houston area's] leading families," as indicated by the fact that Ruth "was a houseguest of Governor and Mrs. William Pettus Hobby when [Ruth] first came from Austin to join the [UH] faculty in 1935" (Nicholson 162). A similar point can be made on a national scale given that by 1937, mother Anna, then president of the Chautauqua Women's Club of New York, invited several prominent women to speak at the club's summer events series. Among the invited speakers were Eleanor Roosevelt and Ruth Pennybacker, and by that time Ruth taught at the University of Houston, a fact noted in publicity for the Chautauqua Women's Club (Suzanne).

Although Ruth lacked her mother's clubwoman record, Ruth's teaching and supervision of student writers at UH, discussed in Chapter Four, show a kinship to her mother's national civic work, a kinship that allows us to see Ruth's approach to teaching and supervising as indebted to her interactions beyond UH. We might remember Ruth's connections to her mother when, for instance, Ruth encouraged her students to write about what they know and when Ruth ensured that even her first-year composition students took their writing public by adding their writing to UH's first literary magazine.

LESSONS FOR LOCAL HISTORIES OF COMPOSITION

In the tradition of the sophists Poulakos describes who prioritized dynaton in their reasoning, I pose the narratives above to emphasize "the known boundaries of the world but [also to urge my audience] to go beyond them" ("The Logic" 21). For me, the "known boundaries" refer to conventions guiding the creation and comparing of local histories of composition: with discipline- or site-specific perspectives and with geographical nearness in mind. My relatively brief re-seeing of these conventions may encounter resistance, as is often the case with proposals of new possibilities (Poulakos, "The Logic" 22). So let me clarify that I intend my reframing of composition, from composition occurring in classes by that name and located in assigned academic buildings, to composition as writing practices involving people who traverse disciplines, professions, and physical places, to be suggestive. It extends Donahue's suggestion about migrating ideas, Drew's metaphor of travelers, and Mauk's point about interacting discursive and material places in an effort to "fire the imagination" of readers about research and teaching possibilities. At the same time, it adds multi-disciplinary layers to recent histories that centralize the role of networks in shaping composition (Mastrangelo). I hope that my reframing complicates readers' understanding of what it could mean to be a student who was refining her language skills for college activities before the 1950s. Among other things, it could mean associating with glocal figures or entities that could include state governments, competing universities, professional and academic fields, and nationally or internationally known leaders. For those of us doing historical research, following movements like the ones illustrated above help us see composition and its affiliates as every bit as complex as we know them to be today—something that the labels *instructor* and *students*, and even *composition*, don't always invite us to examine.

Concerning cross-site comparisons, differences remain between the historical cases of OU and UH, and each kind of historical document can illuminate only part of what happened at any given point in time. But tracking points of contrast can be as generative as studying similarities. For example, a possible rural-urban difference worth exploring further is whether other rural universities pleaded their financial cases to state legislators in the way that OU did and whether other city universities associated with local women's clubs and artistic events in the same way that UH did: was the former a rural phenomenon and the latter an urban phenomenon? Additionally, a pattern suggested by my evidence from both OU and UH is that pre-1950s composition, despite institutional specificity and peculiarity, developed through the work of people beyond English studies and exposed students to multiple disciplinary or occupational groups. In these institutional cases, literacy sponsors who shaped composition, altering what it meant to be a student writing for college credit, consisted of people whose commitments lay in what today would be called a borderland between discipline- and department-specific work and between social and professional work. So if we want to understand how composition grew in the early 1900s, we should treat *composition* as a nexus of interests from the surrounding institution and from broader social, political, professional, and disciplinary configurations. At OU and UH, composition evolved as instructors moved into new roles that included lobbyist, actor, and socialite, and as students found new roles, including teacher and debater.

If applying this pre-1950s information to the present, we should remember that by the 1960s, composition was growing into Composition, to become the field of Rhetoric and Composition. Also, even if our physical surroundings resemble past or present Appalachian Ohio or Houston, Texas, we aren't living in the political environment experienced by OU's William Henry Scott or the social environment experience by HJC student Mary Treadway. However, while heeding these differences, we can notice tensions that circulate across time in higher education institutions. Today, many of us, as instructors and scholars of composition, observe changes in state funding for higher education, as any number of articles in the *Chronicle of Higher Education* attest, and we witness changes to university-community partnerships (e.g., internships, scholarships, service learning). Although organizations such as women's clubs and college debate societies have transformed since the early 1900s, we find new approximations of these entities, or entities that serve a similar purpose as the historical organizations, in non-profit education programs for adult learners and underprivileged teens and in college forensics teams where students write and deliver original orations. To help us investigate which kinds of people and organizations today push college student writing to do new things, rather than drawing only from well-known influences within English and from institutions near or structurally similar to our own, we should ask ourselves: how are our associations, especially our associations outside of Rhetoric and Composition, leading us to people and ideas that follow us back into our classrooms (or to our interactions with composition students in offices, conference rooms, coffee shops, online spaces, or the like)? What historical associations seem worth updating and trying out in a contemporary setting? As I show more fully in Chapter Six, options for re-seeing the work of composition at our college or university may be vaster than we initially think.

CHAPTER SIX
COMPOSITION AS LITERACY, DISCOURSE, AND RHETORIC

As discussed in Chapter One, compositionists' research on place, like their local research on composition history, has been so extensive and varied that it challenges readers to specify the notions of place that they use to undergird their practices. Instructors have long drawn on concepts such as the communication triangle (Kinneavy), the rhetorical situation (Bitzer), and the dramatistic pentad (Burke). In recent decades, some instructors have also or instead drawn on notions of sustainability, interrelationship, and Thirdspace, to name a few of the ideas that have guided Rhetoric and Composition into place-focused research and theory. Simultaneously, detailed descriptions of social, political, and physical places have abounded in local histories of composition, reminding readers that college student writing has existed in more contexts than we usually imagine. Context matters enormously, local histories continue to show us. And conceptions of context, or theories of place, vary widely, other research suggests. So the consumer of these traditions of research is left with the question of how to make the descriptions and theories work for her given the specific institutional, cultural, political, and economic environment in which she works, an environment which, in many cases, may appear to lack the resources needed to support a place-conscious approach to studying and teaching college student writing.

Although my analysis of historical student writing at OU and UH cannot reveal everything that transpired before the 1950s at colleges and universities of other types throughout the country, the analysis can support the construction of flexible modern-day topoi that instructors can use and revise based on the texts available to them and the people, ideas, and places to which the texts allude. Like my experience at OU and UH, many instructors lack hoards of composition essays written by students across the years at their institution. Also, many instructors lack access to extensive notes from other instructors, especially past instructors, and to textbooks and other teaching resources used by their institution in the past. It may even be the case that instructors lack access to historical catalogs or to clear course and program descriptions from catalogs, bulletins, and related documents. However, the presence of these constraints need not prevent the instructor from learning from history about how student writing at her institution has been imbued with meaning, how the writing has done and may still do rhetorical work beyond giving students academic credit. My use of neos-

Chapter Six

ophistic rhetorical theory, here meaning my evocation of concepts with sophistic roots—nomos, kairos, epideixis, and dynaton—for a contemporary purpose, helps me clarify how pre-1950s student writing was situated at OU and UH, and by extension, how student writing at other institutions might be interpreted along similar lines. The kinds of relationships that I unpack between college student writing and its surroundings provide options, ways to look beyond graded student essays, full textbooks, and detailed instructors' notes, for the researcher whose institutional sources are eclectic and unconventional.

By using nomos, kairos, epideixis, and dynaton, I keep in sight an intellectual heritage that encourages the modern-day researcher to embrace multiple narratives to describe composition's spatial work and to decide which narrative is most compelling and useful for her in light of her purposes and her teaching and research environment. Far from an intellectual exercise or game, the pluralization process that I am advocating has real-world benefits. Christopher W. Tindale puts the matter clearly when he analyzes Plato's dialogue the *Euthydemus*. He argues that in this dialogue, the sophists' attempts to keep their fellow speakers "rooted in the labyrinth of words" of their control (Tindale 94) has positive effects because it "encourages 'a sharpness of mind, clarifies problems, and helps to specify and define issues'" (Grimaldi qtd. in Tindale 95). Of course my goal in using concepts with sophistic roots is not to create a "labyrinth of words," but to clarify and specify different avenues by which instructors and scholars can conceptualize how student writing has related, and may still relate, to its surroundings. What results are *kinds* of relationships that may be applied with different effects to a number of postsecondary institutions. It is the job of each researcher to decide which relationship between college student writing and its surroundings holds the most explanatory power given the researcher's texts, students, and institutional history. As Tindale says in his defense of *Dissoi Logoi*, what's important is not to engage with "equally compelling arguments [or, I would add, equally compelling perspectives or interpretations] … as if the matters were beyond resolution. On the contrary it is through the weighing of the contrasting positions that the alleged merits are recognized and the preferred position identified" (104). Although below I expand on what my OU- and UH-based analyses suggest for composition and for the teaching of writing, I leave it to readers to identify what for them counts as their "preferred position[s]."

TERMS AND TEACHING PRACTICES

Based on the historical analyses detailed in Chapters Two through Five, I argue that situating and resituating college student writing in relation to place (i.e., version of place clarified by sophistic ideas) generates useable new perspectives on the writing's rhetorical work. The resituating process allows *composition* to overlap with activities that are usually associated with *literacy, discourse,* and *rhetoric*; the act of writing texts for college approval comes to involve attempts by non-students to make a point as well as attempts by students to achieve multiple goals and reach multiple audiences. Unpacking how this works allows us to accentuate the significance of students' (and faculty's and administrators') involvement in their surroundings and thus the significance of students' connections to literacy, discourse, and rhetoric. In the field of Rhetoric and Composition, one well-known definition of literacy is a process of interpreting and using information in a social context (Brandt 3-4). A widely accepted definition of discourse is language as it is imbued with the ideology (or in Foucauldian terms, power) of a community or culture. A broad definition of rhetoric, since Kenneth Burke and his intellectual successors, is the strategic use of symbols, especially alphabetic symbols, to persuade, create new identifications, or otherwise make a point. Although scholars have tended to treat each of these concepts apart from the others, and at some universities composition drifted away from rhetoric as early as the 1870s, when Harvard's required writing exams decontextualized student writing opportunities and when Alexander Bain's codification of writing influenced American textbooks, I see value in using historical information to put composition into conversation with literacy, discourse, and rhetoric. If focused with conceptual tools that embrace situational fluidity, a blending of categories lets us see student writing relating to others in ideologically managed social and physical places where information is used to further communally understood meaning-making practices—student writing as a literacy practice, a discursive strategy, and a rhetorical act. From this perspective, there is no way to view college student writing as separate from multiple interests, purposes, and audiences, and the responsible instructor can look selectively at the relationships between student writing and its surroundings in order to revise her writing assignments and activities.

Already, some writers of local histories have neared the point of treating writing in conjunction with literacy, discourse, and rhetoric, though ultimately terminological boundaries remain to tell readers how to place the histories into academically recognizable genres. For instance, in *Activist Rhetorics and American Higher Education, 1885-1937*, Susan Kates defines rhetoric as "elucidation in speaking, reading, *and writing*," and she says that she studies rhetoric as opposed to composition "because of [rhetoric's] historical association with philosophies of language" (2, emphasis added). Thus, she treats rhetoric as a broader category than composition and a category that foregrounds one intellectual tradition over another. Another example comes from scholars who frame their local histories as histories of *rhetorical education*, which David Gold defines as "reading, writing, and speaking instruction" (x). Jessica Enoch defines rhetorical education as action that "prepares (or fails to prepare) the student to participate in and contribute to ... civic culture" (152). This capacious term places these scholars' work in a tradition of education-focused rhetoric, as if the spirit of Isocrates is nearby. Meanwhile, in *Local Histories: Reading the Archives of Composition*, editors Patricia Donahue and Gretchen Flesher Moon proceed from the vantage point of *composition* to share historical narratives that stick closely to *the teaching of writing* at specific American postsecondary institutions. More expansively, Deborah Brandt, in *Literacy in American Lives*, and Stephen Parks, *in Class Politics: The Movement for the Students' Right to Their Own Language*, focus on individual people or on educational organizations in a specific time period to make claims about *literacy*, by which they mean people's uses of writing and reading to change their lives or the lives of others, regardless of higher education institutions.

As helpful as it is for local histories to play by genre rules that tell readers from Rhetoric and Composition how to place the histories into clear and often distinct traditions of thought and practice, I maintain that we can learn from a largely untapped source of insight when we examine how even the most formulaic and acontextualized-seeming uses of language, even writing that appears to be nothing more than a college student's attempt to earn a grade (a narrow and, to many people, unattractive conception of *composition*), is also writing that "takes place," to echo Sid Dobrin ("Writing" 11). Pieces that students write for college credit or other approval can bear traces of interest from community members, university leaders, and politicians; and students' writing can look outward or be made to look outward to engage with any number of people, ideas, and places while still serving college purposes. A controlled tracking of connections between college student writing and other forces demonstrates some of how this can be and what it can mean for modern-day teaching and learning. As Chapter Two explains, students can write to push back at institutional codes mandating student behavior. As Chapter Three argues, students can respond through writing to sociopolitical conditions surrounding a university's founding conditions or a university's recently acquired status. As Chapter Four shows, non-students can use student writing to advance an institutional reputation. And as Chapter Five argues, individuals involved with student writing at a university can move through and beyond a single discipline at one postsecondary institution. Each of these relationships supports the notion that context is too fluid a concept to be pinned down, its exact features and various manifestations cataloged and memorized. Some ecological theories of writing account for this (Rice; Cooper), but a sophistic sensibility takes this as its starting point and urges scholars to continually situate and resituate language so as to clarify options and allow audiences to choose the best option for them in light of their purposes and locations.

THE TEACHING OF WRITING TODAY

By sharing ways for scholars and teachers of writing to apply the primary analytical threads from this book to their own institutions, I am assuming that there is value in seeing student writing as composition as well as rhetoric that springs from the intentions and audiences designated by students and/or non-students, composition as well as literacy practices in vogue among members of a particular locale or profession, composition as well as facilitators or co-shapers of city and state discourses. I am suggesting that although students, instructors, and institutions may indeed see the work of student writing as giving students grades and advancing students through their coursework, what students are doing when they write can and should be conceptualized more broadly and pluralistically. Many college faculty members and administrators already see their extracurricular offerings and their internships and other professional preparation options as connected to many surrounding contexts: nearby town or city needs, state requirements, state or national funding sources, local or glocal occupational trends. The writing that college students do, even if for courses whose official descriptions and curricular functions have gone years without modification, is no less connected to its surroundings.

Of course, instructors may need to adjust the teaching suggestions that I discuss in this chapter; differences in student populations, institutional missions, or town-and-gown relations can necessitate the creation of other, perhaps most modest, versions of the teaching practices and learning occasions that I summarize here. Because course overhauls or the addition of new student organizations may be impossible or impracticable for some institutions to implement at the given time, I want to emphasize that small changes to existing courses, assignments, or in- or out-of-class activities can benefit students. Whatever the exact changes made, the point is for instructors and students themselves to re-see writing of all kinds as a spatially rich and multi-contextual activity. Also, I offer suggestions while realizing that gathering and learning from historical texts takes time and effort, time that is often consumed by grading, conferencing, planning classes, attending committee meetings, and the like. As I hope I have shown, universities with short histories and universities that have retained texts other than those typically valued in composition history (texts about layers of context, texts from a variety of perspectives within an institution) can still inform a researcher's sense of the situatedness of student writing at her institution. The researcher need not emulate the historiographical decisions of Albert Kitzhaber's, John Michael Wozniak's, or Robert Connors' historical studies, and need not

Chapter Six

wait for the local history movement to shed light on the researcher's institution or on similar institutions.

Many are the ideas that can be recontextualized to suit the histories and present-day teaching practices of various postsecondary institutions. First, supported by Chapter Two, instructors at numerous kinds of higher education institutions—two-year colleges, technical colleges, women's colleges, historically Black colleges and universities, land-grant institutions, private colleges and universities, recently founded institutions, state flagship universities—can revise their existing assignments and activities to highlight their institution's construction of student identities: the behaviors that students are supposed to show, the goals that students are supposed to have. Using student handbooks, websites, and other institutional literature, students can summarize, describe, respond to, analyze, or critique these constructions. Writing assignments that ask students to examine a social group or, more specifically, that ask students to examine their role within a social group can be paired with writing assignments that ask students to discuss the roles crafted for them by their college or university. Such writing drives home what notions like social construction and performance, via Erving Goffman, can mean for students from the time when they enroll at their institution to the time when they complete program requirements.

Communication Studies professor Ronald J. Pelias sets the stage for this type of inquiry when, in Chapter Three of *Writing Performance: Poeticizing the Researcher's Body* (1999), he foregrounds how students and instructors project a strategic sense of self during the first day of a college class. Tellingly, Pelias titles this chapter "Performing in the Classroom." It would be up to the writing instructor, then, to guide her students through writing activities that bring students into meaningful contact with institutional scripts (not just classroom scripts) that tell students how to behave, what to do and what not to do. Students can keep a dialectical journal detailing their immediate and measured responses to institutional codes for student behavior. Individually or collectively, students can locate themes that emerge across multiple sets of institutional expectations (perhaps comparing historical and current institutional expectations). Student can even try their hand at describing a day in the life of a student who follows the institutional codes perfectly: where must that student go? What must the student spend her time doing? With whom must that student associate, why, and how? Despite the fact that generally colleges and universities, including those of a conservative bent, have relaxed their codes for student behavior in recent decades, institutional expectations persist in guidance that specifies the kind of thinker and social agent that each student is urged to become. Institutional expectations can be studied as a situated text, and students can in turn create texts that suggest alternative or additional behaviors—making modest revisions like the historical students at OU and UH did or proposing sudden and large-scale changes if the case so warrants. An example of the latter proposal could stem from students' realization that some groups of students, such as transgendered students, have been overlooked in behavioral codes that assume two static gender identities. The work that students do to see and re-see institutional expectations for student behavior could comprise the core of a class unit, a major paper, or a food-for-thought exercise.

After students investigate how and with what consequences institutional expectations bear on their daily lives at their institution, the students will be in a better position to consider new or revised behaviors and to consider what new ideas institutional leaders will be likely to heed. This step, which is more appropriate for a composition course whose primary focus is persuasion, brings students into contact with questions such as, what genres best lend themselves to my purposes and my audience? What revisions are important to me and show respect for the institution's construction of student identities? If, as Nathaniel A. Rivers and Ryan P. Weber argue, a text creates effects if it works in concert with many other kinds of texts (195), then students can consider how different genres play off each other within a larger attempt to begin or change an institutional conversation. For example, would a poster (a visual argument) be seen and remembered by students' desired audience? Would a poster reach people in ways that a brochure, an editorial, and an essay on the same topic would not? Not merely academic exercises, writing and research opportunities along these lines prepare students to think and write in terms of organizational discourses and give students practice deciding which strategies will most realistically affect those discourses. From here, transitioning to writing in business or professional contexts (contexts prized by increasing numbers of students in today's business model of higher education) is a small step—a shift in genre and style, from essays to reports and proposals. Whatever its contours, the shift would need to keep in sight the relationship between student writing and institutional nomoi, that is, between student writing and rules that not only clarify the customs expected of members of a society (or organization), but that also imply what the society or organization considers morally right.

The assignment adjustments above could spring from an instructor's review of historical records or just as easily from an instructor and students' shared inquiry into behavioral standards distinguishing their institution during or since its founding. In other words, the instructor who creates opportunities for her composition students to write about institutional subjectivities need not pause her teaching, grading, mentoring, and committee work so that she can spend a semester excavating archived institutional details alone. Particularly with the digitization of archived holdings, options arise for assignments and activities that apply students' primary research, even if focused on a single document or collection, to arguments for the present.

Second, as shown in Chapter Three, instructors who work in different areas—rural, urban, suburban, exurban; physically near sites of political and economic power, far removed from sites of political and economic power—can build on existing writing assignments and activities to encourage students to investigate how academic as well as creative writing forms reach audiences. In addition to writing traditional arguments, students can explore, in writing, class discussions, and other learning arrangements, cases when indirect and artful writing can expose an audience to new perspectives or change an audience's tone or stance on a topic, much as historical OU and Houston-area students used descriptive, personal, explanatory, and persuasive writing to contribute to discussions of state or city concern. For example, taking a cue from critical regionalism (Powell 6-7), students can use academic as well as creative genres to show how a dominant, mass-mediated representation of a region can be rethought, how the region itself can be conceptualized anew. A classical argument can allow students to discuss whether the region's commonly recognized definition and borders withstand scrutiny. However, a story, poem, or other creative piece, perhaps embedded in or mixed with another genre, can be used to depict new configurations of the region—Houston not as a metropolitan region comprising a handful of counties on the Gulf Coast, but, if illustrated by compelling creative portrayals, a branch of American industrial interests intent on extracting natural resources from the Appalachian Mountains and the ocean floor alike (i.e., the Gulf Coast and the Appalachian Mountains as a shared region). A traditional argument may also be used to propose new regional conceptions, but a poetic addition can prompt students to explore how imaginative writing can help writers re-see, or in literary terms, defamiliarize, a common concept. The point is that students show awareness of the rhetorical significance of language typically prized in composition courses, or simply in composition textbooks, and the rhetorical significance of language prized in literature and creative writing courses.

To an extent, today's textbook writers, some of whom also theorize and research composition, have already broken down the concept of argument so that it considers how aesthetic or otherwise artful moves can further an argument. To pick a well-known example, Lester Faigley and Jack Selzer's textbook *Good Reasons: Researching and Writing Effective Arguments* explains components of traditional (classical) arguments as well as narrative arguments, visual arguments, and so on. And instructors have long availed themselves of the literacy narrative assignment, which encourages students to make a point (or an argument) based on vivid details from personal experience about the students' past textual encounters. The mere presence of description or narration does not usually trouble the waters of composition courses. But owing to the long history of inequality between composition and literature in particular (see, e.g., S. Miller), eyebrows are raised if an instructor encourages students to study and write poems or imaginative prose in a class labeled composition. While understandable given longstanding disciplinary tensions between composition and literature at many institutions, this reaction disallows consideration in composition classes of how imaginative writing engages differently, but not arhetorically, with the world. Strategies of symbolism and suggestion can have real-life effects even if they operate within artistic forms, as many a reader of the novel *Uncle Tom's Cabin* and many a viewer of the comedy television show *Saturday Night Live* can attest. However, many compositionists have not yet shown comfort encouraging writing that has been deemed creative, artistic, or literary. So, without inciting a disciplinary rebellion, the composition instructor can push her students to consider the rhetoricity of imaginative writing by including reflective writing assignments asking students to examine how and why activist writing (e.g., editorials, public awareness bulletins) relies heavily on some forms over others, and how and why creative writing may affect audiences differently or reach entirely different audiences. Composition instructors need not create a full course or unit on imaginative writing in order to spur students to examine how textual moves incite wonder, awe, bewilderment, or, sure, understanding. Simply adding occasions for written meta-reflection can give students opportunities to question textual choices and effects while also ensuring that some textual traditions don't escape rhetorical scrutiny.

Moreover, the fact that students from early OU and students in pre-1950s Houston responded to issues of local concern over time and in campus newspapers and other out-of-class literacy sites deserves notice in light of our information age's abundance of writing genres and platforms—websites, blogs, Twitter accounts, Facebook pages, newsletters, and digital and print newspapers, some of which distribute information more widely and quickly than others, and some of which encourage written responses more directly than others. The recent surge in writing and publishing opportunities enhances modern-day students' chances to respond more than once and over time to state or city conversations affecting the students' college or university. Therefore, both the rate and venue of students' written responses to a local issue can become part of students' rhetorical strategy. If a local issue lacks publicity and is likely to persist for some time, students can discuss how to initiate a conversation that will catch people's attention (an ironic Facebook post that students create and share? a satirical story published in a digital magazine?); then students can determine how to explain points that a particular audience should know (in a classical argument that takes the form of an article? In an article that assumes an earlier text will shortly elicit a widespread reaction?). Timing, including calculated periods of waiting, and venue, including non-academic sites of textual production, become factors for students to interrogate.

Third, building on Chapter Four's updating of epideixis, instructors can extend writing assignments and activities beyond the mere production of texts by allowing students to examine uses to which their (or other students') writing has been put: how has the writing been referenced in promotional material about the English or writing department or about the college or university itself? How has the writing been presented for public consumption? How has the writing figured into claims by faculty members and administrators about students? Class discussions can facilitate this inquiry, but students can research, document, and interpret the process as well, not to criticize their academic institution (though responsible critiques should be allowed), but to show awareness of how readers and interested parties extend the lifespan of texts, use the texts to support other arguments. Granted that FERPA protects students from having their personal information or academic work revealed to public sources without the students' written consent, but still instructors ask students if the students will let one or more of their papers be used as model papers in other classes taught by an instructor. Also, it is common for students to submit their writing to competitions where the writing will be judged by experts and referenced at later events, such as award ceremonies. How often do students who consent to these conditions understand the number and kind of audiences that will scrutinize their work, perhaps scrutinize the writing across years or decades if it is preserved publically? How fully do students comprehend the programmatic, institutional, or disciplinary interests supported by their writing as it circulates beyond a single class? With these considerations in play, students in modern-day composition classes can write and make decisions about whether and how to circulate their writing.

Specifically, students can formally or informally publicize a text that they have written and then revisit the text at a later point to see how its meaning has migrated in the hands of respondents and others. As applicable as this step is for texts that circulate online, it need not apply to online writing exclusively. Students who write editorials in a print version of their campus newspaper, essays for a first-year writing competition, or institutionally solicited evaluations of their major, department, or college may find their work summarized, paraphrased, or quoted in promotional material and institutional research bearing the stamp of approval of institutional leaders. That is, student writing might be repurposed insofar as it supports or illustrates a point that others, usually people with more institutional authority, wish to make. Within a unit in a composition class, students can compose a short text, anything from a slogan to a criticism to an argument, and put the text into circulation to see where it goes, whom it affects, how it gets reused in the service of other people's claims. (If time is short, students can study, discuss, and write about the ripples made by another person's text.) In informal, reflective writing, students can track how or whether their text contributes to other people's written exchanges; if the text is not remembered and evoked in other people's writing, then students can examine who else's ideas are and why. Clearly, the type of activity that I am describing highlights the collaborative potential of writing, but importantly, it also highlight how ethos, especially ethos within an institutional or organizational setting, affects which messages circulate widely and persistently. To take a dramatic example, a university president who publishes a comment from a student on a banner displayed across campus will probably have a more powerful effect than a positive reaction in a campus newspaper from one first-year student about another first-year student's article.

Composition perspectives that centralize collage and juxtaposition have begun to foreground the degree to which texts appear and are thereafter used and reused by others (e.g., P. Sullivan). What remains to be seen in composition pedagogy is how well students can put their own writing into circulation to strategically influence subsequent discussions. Remembering the historical OU and UH students who may not have known how many readers would use their writing to judge their institution's worth, I propose the writing activity above with the hope that it keeps students in the picture as informed and potentially active agents as their writing circulates. As time allows in a composition class, students who monitor uses to which their text was put can explore questions such as, how did other people use my text differently from how I used it? To what extent did my text change in appearance, meaning, or context? In these ways, students can chip away at the idea that they alone control their text if the text circulates among readers and perhaps the idea that their writing circulates only within clear, pre-established boundaries.

Fourth, supported by Chapter Five, which poses historiographical options for composition historians accustomed to seeing postsecondary institutions via commonsensical features (e.g., geographical location, institutional type), contemporary instructors can help students articulate associations (we might say identities) of theirs and ours that follow us into the composition classroom and, regardless of intention, shape how we understand and value the work of writing. Although writing instructors, we are not *only* writing instructors, and although we interact with our students, our students are more than *just* students. The dynaton-inspired approach to conceptualizing composition instructors and students that I detailed in Chapter Five sets the stage for pedagogical practices that lean toward Sharon Crowley's constructionist perspective of history—the idea that terms and concepts change based on the time and culture in which they are used (10). Crowley focuses on the history of rhetoric, but her perspective could also apply to the teaching of writing today.

Perhaps, given the mushrooming of disciplinary specializations that has characterized academe since the 1900s, we downplay the significance of our interactions with people from other disciplines, professions, and physical places. But many undergraduate students, especially first-year students, show greater willingness than us in considering how disciplines other than English (experienced via general education requirements) and how their involvement in student clubs, in work outside of academe, and in various social groups inform their understanding of situated language use. To an extent, Jonathon Mauk, in his *College English* essay "Location, Location, Location: The 'Real' (E)states of Being, Writing, and Thinking in Composition," capitalizes on the richness of students' non-academic lives to break down barriers between academic writing assignments and students' home communities. However, what I think deserves more attention is work of this sort from the instructor's end—work from writing instructors to connect composition assignments and activities to other spheres of disciplinary and professional activity that instructors know or have known well. Despite the specialization, some would say the hyper-specialization, of scholarly fields today, instructors who obtained their degrees in Rhetoric and Composition can consider how their work in other capacities—as writing center tutors or magazine or newspaper editors, their time as undergraduate students taking general education classes, their involvement in local or glocal civic organizations that shape their perception of writing—migrates with them into the classroom and enriches their interactions with students about writing. For instructors with degrees outside of Rhetoric and Composition, taking this action may require reflection on their past or present exposure to other sectors of English studies (e.g., linguistics, literature); to other fields, nearly or distantly related (e.g., communication studies, theater, journalism, sociology, or political science); and to other spheres of work (e.g., volunteer work for neighborhood groups or consultations with people in business or industry). Assignments grounded in this point transcend requests for students to investigate a subculture or discourse community; the assignments assume a migration of influence from one sphere of activity to another.

To take a personal example, an activity that I was once involved in as an undergraduate English major who did not yet identify with Rhetoric and Composition was college forensics, generally defined as competitive intercollegiate public speaking and debating. Throughout the last two-and-a-half years of my undergraduate life, I spent my free time writing and rewriting speeches to deliver from memory at speech tournaments held at colleges and universities of various kinds around the country. At the tournaments, I delivered my speeches to multiple judges as well as to fellow competitors and other audience members, and afterward I discovered whether the rankings and scores that I received from the judges were sufficient to advance me to a tournament's final rounds. If so, I would deliver the same speech again, this time preceding or following a more select group of students and in front of a wider audience. After the tournaments, I would receive written comments from the judges, and I would meet with my coaches, usually communication studies faculty members at my college. While today I don't endorse the highly competitive and hierarchical tendencies of college forensics, and while I realize that that activity differs in important ways from writing a paper for composition classes, I can tap into my history of forensics involvement to see how it informs my in-class explanations of audience and context. For instance, the fact that some of the humorous appeals that I used in my after-dinner speeches made positive impressions on judges in the South but not on judges in the Midwest told me about audience analysis and regional differences. The fact that some of the rooms that I spoke in distracted the judges or me told me about the influence of classroom configurations. The fact that the same speech delivered in what I perceived as the same way could yield vastly different audience reactions each time that I delivered it told me that a communication situation could not be replicated perfectly.

Without reproducing forensics culture in the composition classes that I teach, I can discuss my forensics experience as it pertained to my emerging sense of a rhetorical sensibility, and I can encourage my students to develop similar examples. After subsequent occasions for exploratory low-stakes writing, I can ask my students to analyze or develop an argument whose assumptions about purpose, audience, credibility, or adaptability (or any other key feature of rhetoric) stem from the students' involvement in a particular academic, professional, or civic organization. For example, depending on the institution's student demographics, some students could gravitate to writing prompts such as, how has your paid work in an off-campus setting taught you to revise a message so that it has a desired effect? In what ways is that setting similar to and different from the writing that you do for your college composition classes? Other students could gather more experiential raw material in response to questions such as, how does your participation in a social group shape the ways that you compromise and the ways that you consider multiple perspectives in your arguments? Before assigning a writing assignment based on the latter question, instructors would need to ask themselves how well they have modeled reflective thinking and writing about their own participation in a disciplinary, professional, or social group. Much as catalogs from early 1900s OU show composition linking college students to various academic disciplines, composition today can be used to help students see anew the activities (disciplinary and otherwise) in which they participate and the ways that insights gleaned from those activities accompany students into required composition activities. All this is not to say that composition lacks any parameters of its own, but to say that composition, like rhetoric (Leff 62), lends itself to analysis of other activities, resisting isolation from campus and non-campus life. Instructors who create opportunities for students to examine and compare the work of language to structure disciplinary, professional, or social activities are, I think, preparing students to see including classroom writing as another kind of spatially nuanced and rhetorical meaningful activity.

LOCATING WITHOUT LIMITING STUDENT WRITING

As I have argued throughout this book, historicizing college student writing at specific institutions can help scholars and instructors make sense of the locatedness of the writing of their own students, the ways in which the writing relates to people and ideas in its various surroundings. Rather than attempt to account for all of the ways that writing has related, and still relates, to its surroundings, I have applied four lines of analysis to a rural university and an urban university in order to show the explanatory power of sophistic outlooks when applied to pre-1950s college student writing and, in this chapter, current student writing. Future scholars and instructors may rethink these analytical threads or argue for the importance of other lines of analysis. No matter how other scholars proceed, it is important that they refrain from viewing the analytical options before them as fixed, as topoi of the kind that, during and after the period of classical antiquity, hardened into lengthy codes of rhetorical properties and strategies. Any attempt to codify once and for all the many relational qualities of historical or contemporary college student writing is doomed to fail because no context is static. Just as rhetoric considers always shifting situation-based language (or symbols), college student writing relates pluralistically, and perhaps contradictorily, to complex and unfixed surroundings. To some degree, the study of rhetoric has long incorporated the sensibility that I support, for the late twentieth century saw tremendous excitement about the rehabilitation of sophistic concepts to describe rhetorical practices in a contemporary, pluralistic world. But Edward Schiappa then argued—and many scholars listened—that the label *sophistic* was too problematic to use today because it failed to point scholars to a unifying definition of sophism ("Sophistic" 15).

I believe that foregrounding and updating concepts used by individual sophists to put language-based meanings into motion, despite whether the concepts support one overarching definition of sophistic thought, has value for compositionists because the concepts direct us to blind spots in our usual understandings of context, place, situation, or the like. We may already think about institutional context, but not by tracking relationships between student writing and institutional expectations containing moral implications, as an updated version of nomos would have us do. We may already think about state or city politics, but not usually by examining parallels between student writing for academic activities and issues of concern for the students' institution and immediately surrounding region, as an updated version of kairos would encourage us to do. We may already think about public dimensions of student writing, but not by unpacking strategies used by college faculty and administrators to re-present the writing so that it supports other arguments, as an updated version of epideictic practices would allow us to do. We may even be preparing to borrow from Patricia Donahue's suggestions for new kinds of local histories of composition, but we have only begun to study migrations of people and ideas for their ability to link student writing to many social, disciplinary, and physical places, as a historiography guided by dynaton could prompt us to do. If our understanding of college student writing comes from a perception of classrooms, textbooks, and course requirements as fixed in time and space, and if our histories of composition emerge from descriptions of these factors at a specific site, then we can expect our discussions about writing context to be similarly neat and commonsensical. But a generative view of writing contexts unfolds and analytical opportunities for composition historians and instructors arise if we build on concepts with sophistic roots.

As local portraits of student writing in the past and present proliferate, they should be received as attempts to frame writing in some as opposed to many other ways, as accentuating some of writing's numerous, perhaps countless, relationships. Although these relationships will not take the same form at every college and university, noticing patterns—basic kinds of relationships—across geographical regions and institutional types gives us starting points for new research projects and teaching initiatives whether we work at institutions with long-established and generously supported archives or at institutions with eclectic and recently added records. While no historical collection is ever in fact complete, we can gain usable historical and pedagogical insights even if we work with sources that speak primarily to contexts of student writing, for the right tools enable us to treat context as an active and multidimensional component of our work.

WORKS CITED

"The 1941 Harvest." *The Harvest* 6: ii.

"About the Authors." *The Harvest* 6: 80-83.

Anderson, Martha. "Student Drama." *Ohio University in the Twentieth Century: A Fifty-Year History* 1. N. pag.

Anderson, Olive San Louie. *An American Girl, and Her Four Years in a Boys' College*. Ann Arbor, MI: U of Michigan P, 2006. Print.

"Annual Estimates of the Population of Metropolitan and Micropolitan Statistical Areas: April 1, 2010 to July 1, 2012." United States Census Bureau. Web. 1 March 2014.

Antiphon. "*On Truth*, Books I and II." Sprague 212-224.

Aristotle. *Metaphysics, Books VII-X: Zeta, Eta, Theta, Iota*. Trans. Montgomery Furth. Indianapolis, IN: Hackett, 1985. Print.

Athena. 1923. University Archives. Mahn Center for Archives and Special Collections, Ohio University Libraries. Web. 20 June 2014.

Athens County Pioneer Association Collection. MSS51. Mahn Center for Archives and Special Collections, Ohio University Libraries. Print.

Baker, John C. "August, 1950." *Ohio University in the Twentieth Century: A Fifty-Year History* 1. N. pag.

Bawarshi, Anis S. *Genre and the Invention of the Writer: Reconsidering the Place of Invention in Composition*. Logan, UT: Utah State UP, 2003. Print.

Beach, J.M. *Gateway to Opportunity? A History of the Community College in the United States*. Sterling, VA: Stylus, 2010. Print.

"Be Booster." *The Cougar* [Houston, TX] Dec. 1929: 2. University Archives Collection, Special Collections, University of Houston Libraries, Houston, TX. Print.

Berlin, James A. *Writing Instruction in Nineteenth-Century American Colleges*. Carbondale, IL: Southern Illinois UP, 1984. Print.

Bitzer, Lloyd F. "The Rhetorical Situation." *Philosophy and Rhetoric* 1.1 (1968): 1-14. Print.

Bolling, Emma. "Praeludium: An Interpretation of the Educational Endowment from the Cullens." Master's thesis. University of Houston, 1941. Print.

Booth, Wayne C. "The Rhetorical Stance." *College Composition and Communication* 14.3 (1963): 139-45. Print.

Bordelon, Suzanne. *The Rhetoric and Pedagogy of Gertrude Buck*. Carbondale, IL: Southern Illinois UP, 2007. Print.

Boyd, Margaret. *Diary, January 1873 - November 1874*. MS. Series 2, Box 1,

Works Cited

Folder 17. Boyd Family Collection, MSS 15. Mahn Center for Archives and Special Collections, Ohio University Libraries. Print.

Brandt, Deborah. *Literacy in American Lives*. Cambridge, UK: Cambridge UP, 2001. Print.

Brereton, John C., ed. *The Origins of Composition Studies in the American College, 1875-1925: A Documentary History*. Pittsburgh: U of Pittsburgh P, 1995. Print.

Brooke, Robert E., ed. *Rural Voices: Place-Conscious Education and the Teaching of Writing*. New York: Teachers College P, 2003. Print.

Burke, Kenneth. *A Grammar of Motives*. Berkeley, CA: U of California, P, 1969. Print.

Carroll, Lee Ann. *Rehearsing New Roles: How College Students Develop as Writers*. Carbondale, IL: Southern Illinois UP, 2002. Print.

Caskey, Homer J., Joseph B. Heidler, and Edith A. Wray. *College Composition: A Brief Course*. Boston: Ginn and Company, 1943. Print.

Cheney, Helen. "Education." *The Cougar* [Houston, TX] Apr. 1929: 2. University Archives Collection, Special Collections, University of Houston Libraries, Houston, TX. Print.

Clinton, Magdalene. "A Survey of the English Fundamentals Tests of the 1936 Seniors of the Houston College for Negroes." An essay submitted to the English Department in partial fulfillment for the Bachelor's degree. Texas Southern University, 1937. Robert James Terry Lib. Special Collections, Texas Southern University, Houston, TX. Print.

Cochran, J. Chester. "The Municipal University as a Community Service Institution, Especially as Exemplified in the Aims, Organization and Growth of the University of Houston." Diss. University of Houston, 1950. University Archives Collection, Special Collections, University of Houston Libraries, Houston, TX. Print.

The Columbiad. Athens, OH: University Archives, Mahn Center for Archives and Special Collections, Ohio University Libraries, Print.

Connors, Robert J. *Composition-Rhetoric: Backgrounds, Theory, and Pedagogy*. Pittsburgh: U of Pittsburgh P, 1997. Print.

Consigny, Scott. "Gorgias's Use of the Epideictic." *Philosophy and Rhetoric* 25.3 (1992): 281-97. Print.

Conway, Kathryn M. "Woman Suffrage and the History of Rhetoric at the Seven Sisters Colleges, 1865-1919." *Reclaiming Rhetoric: Women in the Rhetorical Tradition*. Ed. Andrea A. Lunsford. Pittsburgh: U of Pittsburgh P, 1995. 203-26. Print.

Cooper, Marilyn M. "The Ecology of Writing." *College English* 48.4 (1986): 364-75. Print.

The Cougar [Houston, TX] Apr. 1929: 1. University Archives Collection, Special Collections, University of Houston Libraries, Houston, TX. Print.

The Cougar [Houston, TX] 22 Nov. 1933: 1. *Houston, Tex.: Houston Junior College, 1928-1934*. Microfilm.

Crowley, Sharon. "Let Me Get This Straight." Vitanza 1-19.

Davidson, Jean. "Special Days and Celebrations." *Ohio University in the Twentieth Century: A Fifty-Year History* 1. N. pag.

Davis, John Merrill. "Margaret Boyd." *Ohio University Bulletin, June 1917*. Ohio University Lib. 8-11. 30 Apr. 2011. Web. 16 Sep. 2013.

"Dear Old College." *The Cougar* [Houston, TX] 25 May 1932: 2. *Houston, Tex.: Houston Junior College, 1928-1934*. Microfilm.

Delpit, Lisa D. "The Silenced Dialogue: Power and Pedagogy in Educating Other People's Children." *Harvard Educational Review* 58.3 (1988): 280-98. Print.

Devet, Bonnie D. "Redefining the Writing Center with Ecocomposition." *Composition Forum* 23 (2011): n. pag. Web. 11 Nov. 2013.

Diener, Thomas, ed. *Growth of an American Invention: A Documentary History of the Junior College Movement*. New York: Greenwood, 1986. Print.

"*Dissoi Logoi*." *The Rhetorical Tradition: Readings from the Classical Times to the Present*. 2nd ed. Eds. Patricia Bizzell and Bruce Herzberg. Boston: Bedford/St. Martin's, 2001. 49-55. Print.

Dobrin, Sidney I. *Postcomposition*. Carbondale, IL: Southern Illinois UP, 2011. Print.

---. "Writing Takes Place." Weisser and Dobrin 11-25. Print.

Donahue, Patricia, and Gretchen Flesher Moon, eds. *Local Histories: Reading the Archives of Composition*. Pittsburgh: U of Pittsburgh P, 2007. Print.

Donahue, Patricia. "Disciplinary Histories: A Meditation on Beginnings." Donahue and Moon 220-36.

"Dramatic Club Gives Banquet at Le Blanc's." *The Cougar* [Houston, TX] 29 Feb. 1934: 1. *Houston, Tex.: Houston Junior College, 1928-1934*. Microfilm.

Drew, Julie. "The Politics of Place: Student Travelers and Pedagogical Maps." Weisser and Dobrin 57-68.

Drum, Mary Lou. "Introduction: 1920." *Ohio University in the 1920s: A Social History*. N. pag.

Ede, Lisa, and Andrea Lunsford. "Audience Addressed/Audience Invoked: The Role of Audience in Composition Theory and Pedagogy." *College Composition and Communication* 35.2 (1984): 155-71. Print.

"Editorials." *The Student's Magazine* 1 (1879). *Ohio University Newspapers II*, reel 1.

Emerson, William Dana. "Athens, Ohio." *The Student's Magazine* 1 (1880). *Ohio*

University Newspapers II, reel 1.

Enoch, Jessica. "Finding New Spaces for Feminist Research." Octalog III: The Politics of Historiography in 2010. *Rhetoric Review* 30.2 (2011): 109-34. Print.

---. *Refiguring Rhetorical Education: Women Teaching African American, Native American, and Chicano/a Students, 1865-1911*. Carbondale, IL: Southern Illinois UP, 2008. Print.

Faigley, Lester, and Jack Selzer. *Good Reasons: Researching and Writing Effective Arguments*. 4th ed. New York: Longman, 2009. Print.

Fairchild, James H. *Oberlin: The Colony and the College, 1833-1883*. Oberlin, OH: E.J. Goodrich. 1883. Print.

Farias, Albert. "I Live in America." *The Harvest* 6: 19-23.

Finnegan, Cara L., and Marissa Lowe Wallace. "Origin Stories and Dreams of Collaboration: Rethinking Histories of the Communication Course and the Relationship Between English and Speech." *Rhetoric Society Quarterly* 44.5 (2014). 401-426. Print.

Fitzgerald, Kathryn. "The Platteville Paper Revisited: Gender and Genre in a Normal School Writing Assignment." Donahue and Moon 115-33.

Fleckenstein, Kristie S. et al. "The Importance of Harmony: An Ecological Metaphor for Writing Research." *College Composition and Communication* 60.2 (2008): 388-419. Print.

"F.M. Black." *The Cougar* [Houston, TX] 6 Apr. 1928: 1, 3. University Archives Collection, Special Collections, University of Houston Libraries, Houston, TX. Print.

Gagarin, Michael. *Antiphon the Athenian: Oratory, Law, and Justice in the Age of the Sophists*. Austin, TX: U of Texas P, 2002. Print.

Gere, Anne Ruggles. *Intimate Practices: Literacy and Cultural Work in U.S. Women's Clubs, 1880-1920*. Urbana, IL: U of Illinois P, 1997. Print.

Gillam, Kenneth. "Writing in Ecological Microcosms: A Pedagogical Field Map for Re-thinking Process." *Open Words: Access and English Studies* 2.2 (2008): 43-66. Web. 20 Sep. 2013.

Glenn, Cheryl, and Jessica Enoch. "Invigorating Historiographic Practices in Rhetoric and Composition Studies." Ramsey et al. 11-27.

Gold, David. *Rhetoric at the Margins: Revising the History of Writing Instruction in American Colleges, 1873-1947*. Carbondale, IL: Southern Illinois UP, 2008. Print.

Goggin, Peter N., ed. *Environmental Rhetoric and Ecologies of Place*. New York: Routledge, 2013. Print.

Gorgias. "*A Defense on Behalf of Palamedes* by the Same Author." Sprague 54-63.

---. "*The Encomium of Helen*." Sprague 50-54.

"Graeco-Syrian Maxims." *Ancilla to the Pre-Socratic Philosophers: A Complete Translation of the Fragments in Diels-Kranz,* Die Fragmente der Vorsokratiker. Trans. Kathleen Freeman. 1948. Cambridge, MA: Harvard UP, 1996. 127. Print.

Greenbaum, Andrea. *Emancipatory Movements in Composition: The Rhetoric of Possibility.* Albany, NY: SUNY P, 2002. Print.

Grego, Rhonda C., and Nancy S. Thompson. *Teaching/Writing in Thirdspaces: The Studio Approach.* Carbondale, IL: Southern Illinois UP, 2008. Print.

Gruenewald, David A., and Gregory A. Smith, eds. *Place-based Education in the Global Age: Local Diversity.* New York: Erlbaum, 2008. Print.

Guthrie, W.K.C. *The Sophists.* Cambridge, UK: Cambridge UP, 1971. Print.

Hahnel, Germaine. "Extra-curricular Clubs." *Ohio University in the 1920s: A Social History* N. pag.

The Harvest, 15 vols, University Archives Collection, Special Collections, University of Houston Libraries, Houston, TX, 1936-50. Print.

Heath, Shirley Brice. *Ways with Words: Language, Life, and Work in Communities and Classrooms.* Cambridge, UK: Cambridge UP, 1983. Print.

Hicks, Nancy Jean, et al. "Introductory Note." *The Harvest* 7: ii.

Hill, Adams Sherman. *The Principles of Rhetoric.* New York: Harper & Brothers, 1878. Revised 1899. Print.

"Historical Population: 1900 to 2013." City of Houston Planning and Development Department. Web. 1 March 2014.

Hobbs, Catherine. "Introduction: Cultures and Practices of U.S. Women's Literacy." Hobbs 1-33.

---, ed. *Nineteenth-Century Women Learn to Write.* Charlottesville, VA: U of Virginia P, 1995. Print.

Holiday, Judy. "Still Sophistic (After All These Years): An Interview with Susan Jarratt." *Composition Forum* 22 (2010). Web. 24 Feb. 2014.

Hoover, Judith D. "'Miners Starve, Idle or Working': Working-Class Rhetoric of the Early Twentieth Century." *Who Says? Working-Class Rhetoric, Class Consciousness, and Community.* Ed. William DeGenaro. Pittsburgh: U of Pittsburgh P, 2007. 32-46. Print.

Hoover, Thomas Nathaniel. *The History of Ohio University.* Athens, OH: Ohio UP, 1954. Print.

"Houston Delphian Scholarship Foundation." Box 4, Folder 47. The Houston Assembly of Delphian Chapters Records, Special Collections, University of Houston Libraries, Houston, TX. Print.

Houstonian 1934. Houstonian Yearbook Collection, Special Collections, University of Houston Libraries, Houston, TX. Web. 10 May 2014.

Howard, Christine G. Kelley. "An Enperiment [sic] in the Teaching of English in the Furney Richardson Rural High School of Teague, Texas, 1935-1936." An essay submitted to the English Department in partial fulfillment for the Bachelor's degree. Texas Southern University, 1937. Robert James Terry Lib. Special Collections, Texas Southern University, Houston, TX. Print.

"Introducing—Our Faculty." *The Cougar* [Houston, TX] 30 Apr. 1928: 4. University Archives Collection, Special Collections, University of Houston Libraries, Houston, TX. Print.

Jarratt, Susan C. *Rereading the Sophists: Classical Rhetoric Refigured*. Carbondale, IL: Southern Illinois UP, 1991. Print.

---. "Toward a Sophistic Historiography." *Pre-Text: The First Decade*. Ed. Victor J. Vitanza. Pittsburgh, PA: U of Pittsburgh P, 1993. 263-82. Print.

Johnson, Nan. *Gender and Rhetorical Space in American Life, 1866-1910*. Carbondale, IL: Southern Illinois UP, 2002. Print.

"Junior College Will Meet Texas." *The Cougar* [Houston, TX] 12 Mar. 1934: 1, 4. *Houston, Tex.: Houston Junior College, 1928-1934*. Microfilm.

Kates, Susan. *Activist Rhetorics and American Higher Education, 1885-1937*. Carbondale, IL: Southern Illinois UP, 2001. Print.

Kelley, Mary. *Learning to Stand and Speak: Women, Education, and Public Life in America's Republic*. Chapel Hill, NC: U of North Carolina P, 2006. Print.

Kerferd, G.B. *The Sophistic Movement*. Cambridge, UK: Cambridge UP, 1981. Print.

Kinneavy. James L. *A Theory of Discourse: The Aims of Discourse*. New York: Norton, 1980. Print.

Kirsch, Gesa E., and Liz Rohan, eds. *Beyond the Archives: Research as a Lived Process*. Carbondale, IL: Southern Illinois UP, 2008. Print.

---. "Introduction: the Role of Serendipity, Family Connections, and Cultural Memory in Historical Research." Kirsch and Rohan 1-9.

Kitzhaber, Albert R. *Rhetoric in American Colleges, 1850-1900*. Dallas: Southern Methodist UP, 1990. Print.

Knox, Helen. *Mrs. Percy V. Pennybacker: An Appreciation*. New York: Fleming H. Revell Company, 1916. 13 Dec. 2010. Web. 4 Feb. 2014.

Leff, Michael. "The Habitation of Rhetoric." *Contemporary Rhetorical Theory: A Reader*. Eds. John Louis Lucaites, Celeste Michelle Condit, and Sally Caudill. New York: Guilford, 1999. 52-64. Print.

Lemon, Hilda Long. "College Deferred." *The Harvest* 3: 1-5.

L'Eplattenier, Barbara, and Lisa Mastrangelo. *Historical Studies of Writing Program Administration: Individuals, Communities, and the Formation of a Discipline*. West Lafayette, IN: Parlor, 2004. Print.

Manley, Bruce. "Junior College Best Preparation for Life of Higher Education." *The Cougar* [Houston, TX] Apr. 1929: 3. University Archives Collection,

Special Collections, University of Houston Libraries, Houston, TX. Print.

Martzolff, Clement L., ed. *Poems on Ohio*. Columbus, OH: Ohio State Archeological and Historical Society, 1911. Print.

Masters, Thomas M. *Practicing Writing: The Postwar Discourse of Freshman English*. Pittsburgh: U of Pittsburgh P, 2004. Print.

Mastrangelo, Lisa. *Writing a Progressive Past: Women Teaching and Writing in the Progressive Era*. Anderson, SC: Parlor, 2012: Print.

Mauk, Jonathon. "Location, Location, Location: The 'Real' (E)states of Being, Writing, and Thinking in Composition." *College English* 65.4 (2003): 368-88. Print.

McComiskey, Bruce. *Gorgias and the New Sophistic Rhetoric*. Carbondale, IL: Southern Illinois UP, 2002. Print.

McKee, Grosvenor S. *Grosvenor S. McKee Scrapbook*. UA00014. University Archives, Mahn Center for Archives and Special Collections, Ohio University Libraries. N. pag. Print.

Meeker, Shannon. "Campus Politics." *Ohio University in the Twentieth Century: A Fifty-Year History* 1. N. pag.

Miller, Susan. *Textual Carnivals: The Politics of Composition*. Carbondale, IL: Southern Illinois UP, 1993. Print.

Miller, Thomas P. *The Evolution of College English: Literacy Studies from the Puritans to the Postmoderns*. Pittsburgh: U of Pittsburgh P, 2011. Print.

"Mitchell Acclaimed as Matinee Idol." *The Cougar* [Houston, TX] 26 Mar. 1934: 4. *Houston, Tex.: Houston Junior College, 1928-1934*. Microfilm.

Mitchell, L. Standlee. *American Literature and the Short Story: [Teaching Materials]*. Houston, TX: U of Houston, 1922. University Archives Collection, Special Collections, University of Houston Libraries, Houston, TX. Print.

Moon, Gretchen Flesher. "Locating Composition History." Donahue and Moon 1-13.

Morris, Kathryn. "Introduction—1900." *Ohio University in the Twentieth Century: A Fifty-Year History* 1. N. pag.

---. "Introduction—1929." *Ohio University in the 1920s: A Social History*. N. pag.

"Mrs. Pennybacker, Club Leader, Dead." *New York Times* 5 Feb. 1938: 15. ProQuest Historical Newspapers. Web. 15 Apr. 2014.

"Mrs. Pennybacker Dies at Age of 76." *The Sun* 5 Feb. 1938: 7. ProQuest Historical Newspapers. Web. 15 Apr. 2014.

"Mrs. Roosevelt Hostess." *New York Times* 3 Nov. 1931: 35. ProQuest Historical Newspapers. Web. 14 Apr. 2014.

Myers, David Gershom. *The Elephants Teach: Creative Writing Since 1880*. Chicago: U of Chicago P, 1996. Print.

Nicholson, Patrick J. *In Time: An Anecdotal History of the First Fifty Years of the University of Houston*. Houston: Pacesetter, 1977. Print.

Notomi, Noburu. *The Unity of Plato's Sophist: Between the Sophist and the Philosopher*. Cambridge, UK: Cambridge UP, 1999. Print.

Oberholtzer, Edison Ellsworth. *The Growth and Development of the University of Houston: A Summation, March, 1927 - May, 1950*. Houston, TX: U of Houston 1950. University Archives Collection, Special Collections, University of Houston Libraries, Houston, TX. Print.

Ogren, Christine A. *The American State Normal School: "An Instrument of Great Good."* New York: Palgrave Macmillan, 2005. Print.

Ohio University in the 1920s: A Social History. Athens, OH: Mahn Center for Archives and Special Collections, Ohio University Libraries, 1950. Print.

Ohio University Bulletin, Undergraduate Catalog, 1843, 1868-1869, 1869-1870, 1872-1873, 1901-1902, 1902-1903, 1906-1907, 1919-1920, 1925-1926, 1940-1941, 1950-1951. Ohio University Libraries. 20 Apr. 2011. Web. 13 Dec. 2013.

"Ohio University Charter." *Ohio University Board of Trustees*. Ohio University, 2014. Web. 29 Jan. 2014.

Ohio University Class of 1873. University Archives, Mahn Center for Archives and Special Collections, Ohio University Libraries.

Ohio University in the Twentieth-Century: A Fifty-Year History 1-2. Athens, OH: Mahn Center for Archives and Special Collections, Ohio University Libraries, 1950. Print.

Ohmann, Richard M. *English in America: A Radical View of the Profession*. New York: Oxford UP, 1976. Print.

"Organizational Information: 1933-1937: Houston Delphian Assembly." Box 1, Folder 2. The Houston Assembly of Delphian Chapters Records, Special Collections, University of Houston Libraries, Houston, TX. Print.

Parks, Stephen. *Class Politics: The Movement for the Students' Right to Their Own Language*. Urbana, IL: National Council of Teachers of English, 2000. Print.

Patterson, N.S. "University for a Community." *The Texas Outlook* 32.6 (1948): 11-12. Print.

Pelias, Ronald. J. *Writing Performance: Poeticizing the Researcher's Body*. Carbondale, IL: Southern Illinois UP, 1999. Print.

Pennybacker, Ruth. "Part I: Introductory Note." *The Harvest* 1: iv.

---. "Part II: Introductory Note." *The Harvest* 1: 34.

---. "Introductory Note." *The Harvest* 2: iv.

---. "Introductory Note." *The Harvest* 3: ii.

---. "Introductory Note." *The Harvest* 4: ii.

---. "Introductory Note." *The Harvest* 6: iii.

"Period to Be Hour and Half [sic] in New Session." *The Cougar* [Houston, TX] 30 Apr. 1928: 1, 3. University Archives Collection, Special Collections, University of Houston Libraries, Houston, TX. Print.

"Personal Paragraphs." *The Cougar* [Houston, TX] 19 Oct. 1934: 3. *Houston, Tex.: Houston Junior College, 1928-1934*. Microfilm.

Peters, William E. *Legal History of the Ohio University*. Cincinnati: Western Methodist Book Concern, 1910. Print.

Plato. *Gorgias*. Trans. James H. Nichols, Jr. Ithaca, NY: Cornell UP, 1998. Print.

---. "*Hippias Major* 282C." Sprague 72.

---. "*Hippias Major* 286A." Sprague 97.

---. "*Hippias Minor* 363C-D, 364A." Sprague 96-97.

Poulakos, John. "The Logic of Greek Sophistry." *Historical Foundations of Informal Logic*. Eds. Douglas Walton and Alan Brinton. Brookfield, VT: Ashgate, 1997. 12-24. Print.

---. *Sophistical Rhetoric in Classical Greece*. Columbia, SC: U of South Carolina P, 1995. Print.

---. "Toward a Sophistic Definition of Rhetoric." *Philosophy & Rhetoric* 16.1 (1983): 35-48. Print.

Powell, Douglas Reichert. *Critical Regionalism: Connecting Politics and Culture to the American Landscape*. Chapel Hill, NC: U of North Carolina P, 2007. Print.

"Preface." *The Harvest* 9: 2.

"Preface." *The Harvest* 10: 4.

"Preface." *The Harvest* 11: 4.

"Preface." *The Harvest* 12: N. Pag.

"Preface." *The Harvest* 13: 3.

"Rambling Reporter." *The Cougar* [Houston, TX] 5 Oct. 1934: 2. *Houston, Tex.: Houston Junior College, 1928-1934*. Microfilm.

Ramsey, Alexis E., et al., eds. *Working in the Archives: Practical Research Methods for Rhetoric and Composition*. Carbondale, IL: Southern Illinois UP, 2010. Print.

"Removal of the College." *The Echo and the University Record*. February, 1843. Historic Ohio University Newspaper Collection. University Archives, Mahn Center for Archives and Special Collections, Ohio University Libraries.

Reynolds, Nedra. *Geographies of Writing: Inhabiting Places and Encountering Difference*. Carbondale, IL: Southern Illinois UP, 2004. Print.

Rice, Jenny Edbauer. "Unframing Models of Public Distribution: From Rhetorical Situation to Rhetorical Ecologies." *Rhetoric Society Quarterly* 35.4 (2005): 5-24. Print.

Ritter, Kelly. "Archival Research in Composition Studies: Re-Imagining the His-

torian's Role." *Rhetoric Review* 31.4 (2012): 461-78. Print.
---. *Before Shaughnessy: Basic Writing at Yale and Harvard, 1920-1960*. Carbondale, IL: Southern Illinois UP, 2009. Print.
---. *To Know Her Own History: Writing at the Woman's College, 1943-1963*. Pittsburgh: U of Pittsburgh P, 2012. Print.
Rivers, Nathaniel A., and Ryan P. Weber. "Ecological, Pedagogical, Public Rhetoric." *College Composition and Communication* 63.2 (2011): 187-218. Print.
Rorty, Richard. "The Historiography of Philosophy: Four Genres." *Philosophy in History: Essays on the Historiography of Philosophy*. Eds. Richard Rorty, J.B. Schneewind, and Quentin Skinner. Cambridge, UK: Cambridge UP, 1984. 49-75. Print.
Royster, Jacqueline Jones. *Traces of a Stream: Literacy and Social Change among African American Women*. Pittsburgh: U of Pittsburgh P, 2000. Print.
Schiappa, Edward. "Neo-Sophistic Rhetorical Criticism or the Historical Reconstruction of Sophistic Doctrines?" *Philosophy and Rhetoric* 23.3 (1990): 192-217. Print.
---. *Protagoras and Logos: A Study in Greek Philosophy and Rhetoric*. 2nd ed. Columbia, SC: U of South Carolina P, 2003. Print.
---. "Sophistic Rhetoric: Oasis or Mirage?" *Rhetoric Review* 10.1 (1991): 5-18. Print.
Schultz, Lucille M. *The Young Composers: Composition's Beginnings in Nineteenth-Century Schools*. Carbondale, IL: Southern Illinois UP, 1999. Print.
Scott, Margaret. "Extra-Curricular Activities." *Ohio University in the Twentieth Century: A Fifty-Year History* 1. N. pag.
Shepperd, Louise. "English Prof Has Praise for College." *The Cougar* [Houston, TX] Apr. 1929: 4. University Archives Collection, Special Collections, University of Houston Libraries, Houston, TX. Print.
Sipiora, Phillip. "Introduction: The Ancient Concept of Kairos." *Rhetoric and Kairos: Essays in History, Theory, and Praxis*. Eds. Phillip Sipiora and James S. Baumlin. Albany, NY: SUNY P, 2002. 1-22. Print.
Smith, Irene Elizabeth "A Survey of Student Custom and Tradition at Ohio University." Master's thesis, Ohio University, 1938. Print.
Soja, Edward W. *Thirdspace: Journeys to Los Angeles and Other Real-and-Imagined Places*. Cambridge, MA: Blackwell, 1996. Print.
Soliday, Mary. *Everyday Genres: Writing Assignments across the Disciplines*. Carbondale, IL: Southern Illinois UP, 2011. Print.
---. *The Politics of Remediation: Institutional and Student Needs in Higher Education*. Pittsburgh: U of Pittsburgh P, 2002. Print.
"Southwestern Authors Will Be Lecture Topic." *Pittsburgh Post-Gazette* 20 Jul. 1931: 8. Google News. Web. 1 June 2013.

Sprague, Rosamond Kent, ed. *The Older Sophists: A Complete Translation by Several Hands of the Fragments in* Die Fragmente der Vorsokratiker *Edited by Diels-Kranz with a New Edition of Antiphon and* Euthydemus. 1972. Indianapolis: Hackett, 2001. Print.
"Staff of the 1943 Harvest." *The Harvest* 8: 2.
Strickland, Donna. *The Managerial Unconscious in the History of Composition Studies*. Carbondale, IL: Southern Illinois UP, 2011. Print.
Sullivan, Dale L. "Kairos and the Rhetoric of Belief." *Quarterly Journal of Speech* 78.3 (1992): 317-332. Print.
Sullivan, Patricia Suzanne. *Experimental Writing in Composition: Aesthetics and Pedagogies*. Pittsburgh: U of Pittsburgh P, 2012. Print.
Super, Charles William. *A Pioneer College and Its Background (The Ohio University)*. Salem, MA: Newcomb & Gauss, 1924. Print.
Suzanne. "Madame Chairman…." *The Washington Post* 4 Aug. 1937: 13. ProQuest Historical Newspapers. Web. 1 June 2013.
Taylor, William Alexander. *The Biographical Annals of Ohio, 1902-1903: A Handbook of the Government and Institutions of the State of Ohio*. Vol. 1. Columbus, OH: 75th General Assembly, 1902. Print.
Temple, Judy Nolte, and Suzanne L. Bunkers. "Mothers, Daughters, Diaries: Literacy, Relationship, and Cultural Context." Hobbs 197-216.
Tindale, Christopher W. *Reason's Dark Champions*. Columbia, SC: U of South Carolina P, 2010. Print.
Toulmin, Stephen. "The Tyranny of Principles." *Readings in Contemporary Rhetoric*. Eds. Karen A. Foss, Sonja K. Foss, and Robert Trapp. Prospect Heights, IL: Waveland, 2002. 93-109. Print.
"Twenty-Six Literary Club Records Minutes, 1922-1929." Box 1, File 4. The Twenty-Six Literary Club Records, c. 1910-1994, MS 66, Woodson Research Center, Fondren Library, Rice University, Houston, TX. Print.
Tyler, Carol. "Academic Clubs." *Ohio University in the 1920s: A Social History* N. pag.
University of Houston Administration. *The Statistical Report of the Student Personnel, 1934 to 1944*. University Archives Collection, Special Collections, University of Houston Libraries, Houston, TX. Print.
"U.T. Debators Lose to H.J.C." *The Cougar* 30 Apr. 1928: 1. University Archives Collection, Special Collections, University of Houston Libraries, Houston, TX. Print.
Varnum, Robin. *Fencing with Words: A History of Writing Instruction at Amherst College during the Era of Theodore Baird, 1958-1966*. Urbana, IL: National Council of Teachers of English, 1996. Print.
Vitanza, Victor, J. *Negation, Subjectivity, and the History of Rhetoric*. Albany, NY:

SUNY P, 1997. Print.

---, ed. *Writing Histories of Rhetoric*. Carbondale, IL: Southern Illinois UP, 1994. Print.

Walzer, Arthur E. "Rhetoric as a History of Education and Acculturation." Octalog III: The Political of Historiography in 2010. *Rhetoric Review* 30.2 (2011): 123-25. Print.

Webb-Sunderhaus, Sara. "When Access Is Not Enough: Retaining Basic Writers at an Open-Admission University." *Journal of Basic Writing* 29.2 (2010): 97-116. Print.

Weidner, Heidemarie Z. "Silks, Congress Gaiters, and Rhetoric: A Butler University Graduate of 1860 Tells Her Story." Hobbs 248-63.

Weisser, Christian R., and Sidney I. Dobrin. "Breaking New Ground in Ecocomposition: An Introduction." Weisser and Dobrin 1-9.

---, eds. *Ecocomposition: Theoretical and Pedagogical Approaches*. Albany, NY: SUNY P, 2001. Print.

Welsch, Kathleen A. "Thinking Like *That*: The Ideal Nineteenth-Century Student Writer." Donahue and Moon 4-37.

White, Eric Charles. *Kairomania: On the Will-to-Invent*. Ithaca, NY: Cornell UP, 1987. Print.

White, Jacqueline Ann. "An Historical Study of the Forensics Program at Ohio University from 1812 to 1860." Master's thesis. Ohio University, 1969. Print.

Williamson, J.E. Letter. Box 4, Folder 2. The Houston Assembly of Delphian Chapters Records, Special Collections, University of Houston Libraries, Houston, TX. Print.

Witt, Allen A., et al. *America's Community Colleges: The First Century*. Washington, D.C.: American Association of Community Colleges, 1994. Print.

Zebroski, James Thomas. "Hidden from History: English Education and the Multiple Origins of Contemporary Composition Studies, 1960-2000." *Composition's Roots in English Education*. Ed. Patricia Lambert Stock. Portsmouth, NH: Boynton/Cook, 2012. 26-50. Print.

GLOSSARY

Archive: here used to refer to a collection of historical documents, usually but not necessarily a collection held and controlled by a college, university, or other institution

Composition: here defined as writing completed by college students for formal credit or other academic approval

Dissoi Logoi: different or opposing arguments; the title applied to an ancient and anonymously authored sophistic text featuring diametrically opposed statements

Dynaton: the possible; a state of being located between the actual and the ideal; may appear as *to dynaton* or *dunaton*; cognate with *dynamis*

Ecological Theories of Rhetoric: conceptions of rhetoric as interacting continuously with social, discursive, and natural phenomena

Elocution: the study of speech, with special attention paid to physical qualities such as voice and gestures; elocution was commonly taught in American colleges and universities in the nineteenth century and the early twentieth century

Epideictic Rhetoric: Aristotelian category of rhetoric usually distinguished from the categories of forensic and deliberative rhetoric, and associated with language that praises or blames; speech common for ceremonial purposes

Epideixis: ancient use of language that emphasized display

Historical Reconstruction: according to Richard Rorty's "The Historiography of Philosophy: Four Genres," the privileging of historical understandings when studying information from a past time period

Junior College: category common in late-nineteenth-century to mid-twentieth-century America and used to describe postsecondary institutions that attended to nearby business, industrial, and social needs; offered academic training needed by students to do professional or semi-professional work; and prepared students to transfer to institutions conferring bachelor's degrees

Kairos: the opportune time for communicating in a certain manner

Literary Societies: college student groups devoted to the study of literature and to the study and practice of competitive, and frequently intercollegiate, speaking and debating; literary societies were popular in America in the nineteenth century, especially in the antebellum period, and influenced civic opinion; sometimes the term also referred to non-collegiate speaking or debating groups

Neosophistic Rhetorical Theory: a late-twentieth-century-originated category of theory that mines ancient sophistic ideas from current vantage points and for contemporary purposes

Nomos: a formal rule or informal expectation governing behavior and, in a sophistic tradition, tied to the moral code held by members of a specific culture or community

Normal College (or Normal Department): an academic institution (or branch of an academic institution) offering studies in teacher training, especially in the late nineteenth century and early twentieth century; individual cases varied, but many normal colleges began as "normal schools," which focused on pre-college education

Rational Reconstruction: according to Richard Rorty, the privileging of current understandings when studying historical information

Recitation: in nineteenth-century American colleges and universities, a student's recall of recently taught information

Sophistic Rhetoric: phrase used by some twentieth- and twenty-first-century scholars to synthesize a range of ancient teachings that eschewed certainty and absolute truth in favor of contingent arguments

Women's Clubs: selective civic groups common in the early twentieth century and giving American women opportunities for individual cultivation and civic engagement, as well as participation in parliamentary procedure

www.ingramcontent.com/pod-product-compliance
Lightning Source LLC
Chambersburg PA
CBHW021859230426
43671CB00006B/447